In a Country Garden
Life at
Ravenhill Farm

Seasonal Vignettes,
Recipes and Gardening Tips

Noël Richardson

Whitecap Books
Vancouver/Toronto

Edited by Carolyn Bateman
Proofread by Elizabeth McLean
Cover Design by Designgeist
Interior design by Warren Clark
Cover photograph by Andrew Yeoman
Drawings by Catherine McAvity
Typeset by Warren Clark
Printed in Canada

Canadian Cataloguing in Publication Data

Richardson, Noël, 1937–
   In a country garden

   ISBN 1-55110-399-0

   1. Richardson, Noël, 1937– 2. Farm Life—British Columbia—
Vancouver Island. 3. Cookery (Herbs) I. Title.
S522.C2R52 1996   630'.9711'2   C95-911138-7

The publisher acknowledges the assistance of the Canada Council
and the Cultural Services Branch of the Government of British Columbia
in making this publication possible.

To the memory of my father Ted Richardson, a columnist himself,
who first inspired me to write a column and to Rhonda May,
publisher and editor of *CityFood,* who has given me
such encouragement.

Contents

Contents

Foreword

hen we asked Noël Richardson to write the column "Cooking from the Garden" for *CityFood,* we had only a few simple guidelines for her to follow. "Tell us what your life is like at Ravenhill Herb Farm," we said, "and give us the real dirt. Do it as if you were writing a letter to old friends who love the place as you do but for some reason are never able to get there themselves."

This was more for our clarification than it was for hers. For in our opinion, everyone who does the nine-to-five rat decathlon in the big city needs to get a letter now and then from a friend like Richardson. The blissfully pastoral life that she shares with her husband Andrew Yeoman—as well as an extended family of sheep, donkeys, peacocks, chickens, dogs, cats, stray relatives, and other assorted animalia—may be the perfect stress buster for our times. After all, who needs Valium when you can gaze at apple orchards in bloom? Sheep are not in need of constant ego stroking. And a rosemary bush that is a good listener may be a less conventional therapist, but hey, its advice is probably just as useful and it doesn't charge nearly as much as the guy with the big office.

Thinking too much about life at Ravenhill can make life seem unfair. In the morning, while we are grimly commuting in the pounding rain towards our office cubicles, grinding gears and dental work all the way, Noël Richardson is lazily leaning over her daffodil-yellow sink, pouring herself a second cup of coffee, and contemplating the misty view of the bedding plants from her kitchen window. And at lunchtime, while we are standing in line at the Food Fair madhouse to get our Styrofoam plate of micro-waved Combination B, Richardson is strolling through the garden plucking a sun-ripened tomato from the vine and garnishing it with a pinching of baby tarragon leaves. This woman actually has such things as hammocks, rowboats with shade umbrellas, and birdbath/sundials in her life.

In short, she lives the life that Martha Stewart would live if Martha Stewart had a life. But knowing Noël, she would thoroughly object to being portrayed as, to use her words, "one of those lacy, laudanum-stoned women" lounging around on the pages of *Victoria*. And she'd be right (although she has been featured in that magazine). The fact is, both she and Andrew Yeoman are hard-working, denim-clad gardeners and their generosity in sharing the daily details of their lives has sometimes come at a cost to their privacy. As experienced one early summer morning when Richardson sat, still clad in nightgown and curlers, on the back porch steps shelling peas and up the driveway rumbled a carload of autograph-seeking, instant camera-popping *CityFood* readers determined to find out if Noël Richardson was indeed fact or fiction.

The couple's generosity extends in other ways as well. Having such a herbal bounty to draw upon, Richardson is an accomplished and sensual cook, as verified by those of us who have tried her recipes and who have invited themselves to her place for lunch. As you might expect, Richardson actively promotes the idea that everything tastes better with herbs—but even she has limits. As she said one day, "I've put herbs on everything—cereal, ice cream, everything—but then one day I caught myself running out to get a sprig of fresh thyme to snip over the dog's dinner and I said "Whoa now, Noël, that's going a bit too far."

We don't agree. Richardson's eccentricities—whether she is practicing donkey psychology, peacock calling, or growing zucchini dirigibles—are what give her columns their unique charm. We appreciate her wonderful wry sense of humor and her candid eye for capturing the small details that have more truth in them than the grand philosophical statements ever do. Her graceful, poetic way of expressing it all has made her a favorite with our readers and we are delighted that, thanks to this book, her writing will be enjoyed by many more people. We get inquiries about the column from around the country—some of them under amusing misconceptions. A man in Nova Scotia mistook the gender of her name and assumed that she and Andrew were decadent gay lovers. A woman in northern Quebec was under the impression that Ravenhill Farm was some sort of vegetarian mental sanitarium and wanted to know if she could send her mother-in-law there.

Well, perhaps she wasn't that far off. After all, what could be more sedative than a stroll through the gardens while sipping a nice cup of herbal tea? What other retirement could be a better reward for a lifetime of effort? Like any other jittery, over-caffeinated editor, I have my escape fantasies too and one day when this job gets the better of me, I might, just like the resident barn owl, hoot around in the Ravenhill rafters myself.

—Rhonda May

Editor and Publisher, *CityFood Magazine*

Preface

very Sunday evening, all through my childhood and teenage years, I watched my father type his weekly column on his old Remington typewriter for the *Courtenay Free Press*.

His column was called "Demos," which, roughly translated, means the voice of the people. For many years he wrote anonymously and the identity of Demos remained a secret. Gradually, though, the locals found out and often on Halloween a big painted sign inscribed with "Demos" would be stuck on our white gate. Demos took on anybody and any institution he felt was not doing the right thing for the community. These included the school board (who were his employers for he was the local school principal), the town council, or even the newspaper for which he wrote.

This Sunday evening ritual often began with father asking mother for some ideas. Then he would go to his desk and peck away at the typewriter for an hour and hand it in the next day on the way to school.

Here I am, fifty years later, writing a monthly column on my Macintosh PowerBook and I wonder how much this early image of father at his Remington influenced me and pushed me towards wanting to have my own column. Now, after three years of writing monthly Cooking from the Garden columns for *CityFood,* I am thrilled to have them collected together in a book.

They are not world-shaking essays, but I hope my observations of our country life have entertained, amused, and perhaps bemused the urban readers of *CityFood*. I think we all carry in our souls an atavistic, Edenic fantasy that goes back to our earliest primitive rural beginnings—perhaps even to the original Eden in some form.

However, many people would much rather *read* about country life as it is cleaner and freer of odors than the real thing. No whiff of chicken house, or raunchy pungent compost heap, or slimy goose mess near the pond. Realizing that one doesn't have to deal with the nitty-gritty of country life adds a touch of relief to the reader's experience.

There is a long tradition of writing about country life in English and American literature, for observing nature reminds us of the old, eternal verities of birth, life, and death. And perhaps it is good for us to ponder these subjects occasionally.

I have enjoyed immensely writing about Ravenhill Farm, the garden, the animals, and about cooking. I would like to thank Andrew Yeoman for creating the garden and giving me a wonderful source of things to write about and being such a good life companion. Also Rhonda May, the publisher of *CityFood*, for asking me to write this column and suggesting I write the way I talk. This was a very validating suggestion. Also thanks to Carolyn Bateman, a truly wonderful and sympathetic editor who first wrote to me and said the essays should be in a book. Finally, thanks to my father Ted Richardson for being such a great role model for a young child. I wish he could have lived to read them and I hope they would have made him smile.

March Comes in
Like a Lamb

he lambs have arrived! All that wishing and waiting and watching has rewarded us. They are now two weeks old and bouncing and prancing around the meadow on the new grass. Getting ready for lambing in late January entails cleaning up the barn and making small lambing pens with portable fences called hurdles. The little pens are filled with heaps of clean golden straw (which will later go to the compost heap). Molasses is bought for the ewes, who drink it mixed with a bucket of warm water right after birth. It gives them quick energy and supposedly helps the milk to flow. The heat lamp is dusted off, ready to use in case the temperature dips. Then once all the preparations are complete, there is nothing to do but watch and wait.

Out my kitchen window, I can keep an eye on our expectant mothers. Two signs of imminent birth are lack of appetite and a moving away from the flock in search of higher ground and a more protected sanctuary. One year I noticed a ewe had separated off and I found her in a corner of the meadow with two just-born lambs. We carried the two wet bundles to the barn with mama following close behind bleating anxiously. We tucked them into the maternity ward and in half an hour the lambs were licked clean and standing up to suckle. Often, in as little as two days, the family is out for the day and put in at night in case of marauding dogs and, of course, so we can collect the manure for the gardens. The spring dance of life begins in the field once again.

In the garden, this is also a month of reproduction, a month of division and multiplication. A bed of tarragon, looking like a miserable pile of dead sticks with the tiniest flecks of green here and there, is actually ready to be divided. Each plant will make ten or more new plants. By March I am longing for the taste of fresh tarragon as it has been denied me since November. I plan a Sunday dinner with a plump organic chicken stuffed with tarragon. I loosen the breast skin and stuff it with snips of new leaves. I put some in the cavity and place some under the bird so it roasts on a perfumed bed. I rub the bird with olive oil and splash some dry vermouth over it to make extra pan juices.

Chives are my second favorite spring herb and the chive plants are also divided this time of year. The farm opens the first Sunday in April and there must be lots of potted-up plants for eager customers who come to replenish their herb gardens and to see the lambs and the hundreds of daffodils. Sometimes Andrew brings me a pot of chives for the house. The warmth forces them on and there is a shorter wait. Chives are the stalwart backbone of herbal cooking and easy to grow. They stay in your garden forever and take only a brief winter vacation. As soon as they bloom you clip them back, fertilize and water, and in a few weeks you will have a tender new crop. Do not waste the chive flowers. Their garlicky sweet pungency can add flavor and color to your dinners. One plant is certainly not enough for a serious cook and chive fancier; a row of four to six plants makes a pretty edging to a flower garden or a lettuce patch, a potager as the French call it.

Lettuces and greens are planted in March: little romaines, 'Tom Thumbs', arugula, mustard greens, oak leaf, and 'Lollo Rossa', which looks like ladies' frilly lingerie. This year the garden provided greens until Christmas, when a frost nipped them. A cold frame would have saved some, but there are times when the frost sneaks up when you are not being observant.

As I explore the garden in March, I brush away the leaves and observing carefully I find all sorts of signs of new herbal growth. Tiny lemon balm leaves are forming and as my fingers brush them the clear lemon scent rushes up to my nose. The mint beds are returning to life, and through the gray twigs of the Greek oregano bed I can see the hot spicy leaves unfurling. The beds will be clipped and groomed and have compost sprinkled on them to encourage their growth. I get down on my knees to see if there is any sign of asparagus—but, alas, nothing yet. With a touch of heat the asparagus tips will soon push up through the covering of manure and compost that has cozily blanketed the roots all winter. Right now all I can harvest is the rich rank smell of mother earth. There are a few brilliant orange and yellow calendulas bordering the asparagus bed. The cheerful jolts of color please the eye in what still seems to be a mostly dormant garden. Calendulas (pot marigolds), named like many plants after the Virgin Mary, have cheered humans for centuries with their color, healing qualities, and nutritional pleasures. You can throw the petals into rice dishes for a poor man's saffron. Soap and salve makers often add the petals to their products. Because they generously self-sow, they are an asset to any garden.

Shallots, garlic, peas, and broad beans (favas) planted in October and November are showing green tips. They are fertilized with compost to give them a spring tonic. There are even some leftovers in the garden, some carrots, beets, and leeks. I make an earthy goodbye-to-winter soup that should give the gardener new strength for all the work ahead. If the sorrel leaves have sprouted, I add some to the soup for a lemony hit. Belgian endive, which has been malingering under sawdust and is a much-needed vegetable in March for salads and hot dishes, will be developing its blanched pointed heads soon. The purple sprouting broccoli is flowering, and I steam the blossoms and serve them on pasta with a touch of anchovy and garlic.

Lest readers think I just glean for edibles in the garden, I look around to see what else there is to observe. My gaze immediately falls on the masses of snowdrops under one of the oak trees. And in a small bed by a stone wall near the goose pond are the tiny yellow aconites that last summer hurled their seeds over the wall; now the wild grass beside the wall is scattered with yellow blossoms.

Five peacocks stalk past me. Fanny and Alexander, the parents, as well as the three offspring who survived the winter and escaped being dinner for the dreaded raccoons, stalk single file through the garden for they are longing for new greens too. I hear the gardener calling and sending the dogs after them. The peacocks take to the air and fly over the fence hooting their piercing alarm calls. The dogs never get near them and the game goes on all summer.

Soon the male peacock, his hormone level rising, will start his very early morning mating cry—much to the dismay of house guests. He fans his tail and does his formal courtly dance around Fanny, who often looks bored and bemused. Something must happen when we are not observing for in May Fanny flies to the loft in the barn and sits on eggs for a month. In late July, Alex's hormone level drops and so do his feathers. It is a tradition at the farm that visiting children may take home any feathers they find. This leads to excited feather hunts in the back meadow and in the barn. I have read about the eating of peacocks in medieval times but have met only one person who ever ate one. A beautiful elderly Scottish cousin, who had many husbands and lived in Ceylon as a tea planter's wife, described hunting trips in the jungle where the beaters killed a hen peacock for the evening pot. Quite delicious she said, though she never told me the recipe.

The geese also have spring fever and the one female (she has four husbands) has begun to lay in a hidden corner behind an old white enamel bathtub once used for watering stock. She does not like being observed and hisses furiously at me if I go near her to see how many eggs she has laid. I will try to check the nest when she is off having a walk or a bath. About the first of May she will start to sit. She lines her nest with goose down, which she pulls from her own breast—to me the ultimate motherly sacrifice. I have read goose eggs make great cakes and omelets but so far have stuck to my chickens, being an egg conservative.

March is truly a month of birth, rebirth, division, and multiplication in the plant and animal world. There are amazing things to observe, and the cook and gardener need to keep close to the ground for it is there they will find an amazing world just ready to burst forth. Raise your glasses high and drink to spring and life!

Simple Roast Tarragon Chicken

1 roasting chicken (a Cornish game hen or frying chicken will also work)
2 bunches of fresh-picked tender tarragon leaves
3 Tbsp. (45 mL) of olive oil
1/2 cup (125 mL) vermouth (dry white)

Wash roasting chicken with cold water and pat dry with paper towels. Place in an ovenproof baking dish.

Loosen the breast skin and push some of the tarragon leaves under the skin. Place a small handful of leaves in the cavity. Place remaining leaves under the chicken. This will flavor the pan juices. Rub the outside of the chicken with the olive oil. This makes the skin crisp. Pour the vermouth over the chicken.

Roast in a 400°F (200°C) oven for 1 to 1 1/2 hours. Add more liquid, either water or vermouth, to the pan if the juices are drying up. Baste every 15 minutes.

Wiggle legs to see if chicken is done; they should be loose and the juices in the chicken should run clear when pricked. Place on a platter and surround with some fresh tarragon. Skim fat off pan juices and serve with mashed or new potatoes and perhaps little green peas. Serves 4.

Broccoli Florets Over Pasta

1 cup (250 mL) lightly steamed garden-fresh broccoli florets (purple or store-bought broccoli is fine)
2 Tbsp. (30 mL) olive oil
2 or 3 garlic cloves finely minced
2 or 3 anchovies rinsed and finely chopped
1/2 cup (125 mL) chicken stock
Fresh grated Parmesan

Steam broccoli and set aside. Place olive oil in a heavy-based frying pan and heat. Cook garlic gently for a minute or so. Add chopped anchovies and stir in with garlic. Stir in chicken stock and cook until it bubbles. Toss in broccoli and stir in well. Serve over cooked pasta and sprinkle with some fresh grated Parmesan and a few grinds of fresh ground pepper. Serves 2.

My Father's Garden

"Nostalgia," my editor said, "that is the theme of the next issue. Early seventies and what we were eating then." I realized right away that being a couple of decades older than my editor, I was not the least bit nostalgic about the early seventies. My nostalgic period is the forties and fifties, when going to a restaurant, for my family, was unheard of. But there was a vegetable garden so laden with nostalgic memories I felt I had to return to those bean rows of long ago.

I began my trip down memory lane with a visit to my *Webster's* to look up "nostalgia." "A sentimental memory or longing for things of the past," it stated. Or, "a form of melancholia caused by a prolonged absence from one's home or country." I proceeded to the *OED* with my magnifying glass and found that the source of the word nostalgia is two Greek words, "home" and "pain." Nostalgia was described in vividly strong terms—a soul sickness, a pathetic insanity, a perplexing indisposition. Clearly, the modern meaning of nostalgia had lightened up over the years and now had a more frivolous tone. A yearning for beads and bell-bottoms of the sixties or for the meatloaf, mashed potatoes, and Kraft dinner that Mom used to make.

For the next few weeks I kept musing on nostalgia and the vegetable garden of my childhood. One day, I found myself doodling, and a rough sketch of the garden appeared on my paper.

There were the raspberry canes against the fence, the rows of corn, the lumps of rhubarb in stalwart formation next to the dustbin, the rows of peas and beans, the strawberry patch, the neglected corner where the Jerusalem artichokes grew year after year, always ready to make desperation soup when all else failed. In the center of this L-shaped garden was the fenced chicken run. Every spring the chicken house got its annual cleaning and the litter was spread on the garden along with horse and cow manure. On very rainy days, the duck pond flowed over into the rhubarb and fertilized the water simultaneously—a natural organic act.

Spring in the garden began with an annual ritual. A man called Elmer brought over a Rototiller and plowed up the garden. The arrival of Elmer was an auspicious event. Father actually became excited at the cultivation of soil and would then plant the wooden cold frame with lettuces and radishes. This excitement sparked a response in us children for father was famous for his English reticence.

After I had drawn my vegetable garden map, I began to make a list of vegetables that were grown in the garden and then made a list of vegetables in our garden now. The early list was very basic and very Waspish. No arugula, eggplant, hot peppers, artichokes, or even a zucchini. Instead, my father grew huge, watery, pale yellow marrows that thrived and grew large at the edge of the compost heap. One year, a marrow grew to forty-five pounds (twenty kilograms) and won a five dollar prize at the Comox Valley Fall Fair for largest marrow in show. Mother had two recipes for marrow—boiled until mushy with a floury white sauce poured over it, or stuffed with sausage meat and cooked. Hardly nineties cooking and difficult to be nostalgic about. Broad beans were grown and interestingly are still loved by Englishmen and Italians, who call them favas. Delicious when young and raw or barely simmered, they are truly disgusting when old, tough-skinned, large, and overcooked.

Father grew peas, beans, carrots, tomatoes, beets, asparagus, cucumbers, and tomatoes. When harvested in mid-summer they were mostly bottled for winter. Mother would railroad the four of us into vegetable preparation, and we would sit in the shade of the Douglas fir trees and cut up vegetables that she processed in glass jars in a huge blue enamel canner on the old McClary oil stove. This was serious business, putting up food for winter, not just for economic reasons but because there was a scarcity of fresh vegetables in the shops during the winter. No vegetables were shipped from Mexico and California. I remember salads in winter were always cabbage, grated carrot, and apple with a homemade boiled mayonnaise. Lettuce was not seen until spring when Father harvested his first crop from the cold frame—tender, limp, leaf lettuce and small crunchy radishes. This was a ceremonial occasion. The salad was dressed with my grandmother's recipe—some cream with a dash of vinegar, pepper, and a small amount of sugar— which left a lovely rich-sweet-tart taste on the tongue.

The bottled vegetables were stored on shelves in a cupboard under the stairs and not eaten until late fall. I loved hiding in this dark, angular space and looking at the jars of rosy beets, green beans, and orange carrots glowing in the under-stairs gloom. I suppose the sight of future dinners was comforting for me. Children in large families are often anxious about the amounts of food they will get. Very early, I learned to watch the server carefully and to count such things as sausages, rolls, cobs of corn, and cookies. Recently, three of us were sharing a platter of oysters in a posh restaurant. I quickly had them counted and allotted.

What did vegetables taste like in those far-off days? In a word—mushy. Canned vegetables always had a boiled, soft texture. My mother's idea of cooking fresh vegetables was to put them to boil at 4:00 P.M. and eat them at 6:00 P.M., whether they were done or not. Occasionally, she would become absorbed with her garden or painting and put the vegetables on very late and I would have this vegetable epiphany: vegetables do not have to be mushy, they can be crisp, crunchy, and delicious. As a consequence, I have rarely cooked fresh peas since I have had my own kitchen. To me, a basket of just-picked peas and a glass of white wine is the perfect pre-dinner happening. To round out the experience, my old sheepdog Emily likes to sit beside me and eat the pea pods as I shell the peas.

Food for most families in the forties and fifties was fuel. It was plain and simple—not a sensuous art form. There was a more puritanical, pragmatic approach to cooking. I can recite like a litany the weekly menu—Roast Beef Sunday, Cold Beef Monday, Shepherd's Pie Tuesday, Pork Chops Wednesday, Sausages Thursday, Fish Cakes Friday, Baked Beans Saturday. The roast beef on Sunday, surrounded by roasted potatoes and home-canned vegetables, was an atavistic tribal occasion. We gathered around the slaughtered animal (roast beast we called it) and no one worried about cholesterol. We loved the crispy fat and the comforting mush of vegetables and gravy. Father and Mother would each be at opposite ends of the table. The worse your table manners, the closer you sat to Father. Gigglers were sent to the kitchen. Mother was rather laissez-faire about table manners and mopped up gravy with slices of bread, which drove Father into a frenzy. Cries of "use the butter knife" and "do not be a savage" still echo down the years.

Now my vegetables are often raw, or crisp, roasted or grilled and marinated. Our garden is full of ethnic treasures such as red and yellow peppers, arugula, endive, cardoons, artichokes, yellow and plum tomatoes, tiny French beans, shallots, and garlic. Garlic never touched my lips until I left home, and I never met a zucchini until the early sixties.

Vegetables have taken a more central place at the dining table. Today, we gather around a huge platter of grilled vegetables with aïoli mayonnaise. The one vegetable I am still nostalgic about is the potato. This I do not eat raw but love it baked, mashed, roasted, or French fried. I found a Madame Benoit recipe in the sixties for mashed potatoes that I still use. To the cooked mashed potatoes add a big dollop of butter, lots of fresh ground pepper, 1/2 cup (125 mL) finely chopped parsley, and enough milk to make it creamy. This kind of "mush purée" is worth being nostalgic about.

Freud once wrote that we re-create our childhoods in adult life and certainly I have attempted that with variations. My parents' vegetable garden forms a basis of memories and taste pleasures that have helped me and my gardener husband Andrew create our farm. What we have created is a small paradise filled with rows of beautiful vegetables, redolent compost heaps, herbs intertwined with flowers, chickens, sheep, even a goat and a donkey. Andrew brings in baskets of vegetables for dinner, which are usually served with the crunch left in them. But sometimes I put new potatoes on to boil and wander out to pick mint and get distracted just like my mother did. I return to find the potatoes a little mushy, and when I eat them I smile and think of the vegetable gardens of my childhood.

Sunday Family Pot Roast
with Vegetables and Horseradish Sauce

1 4-lb. (2-kg) pot roast (chuck or round)
Salt and pepper to taste
1/4 cup (60 mL) flour for dredging the roast
3 Tbsp. (45 mL) vegetable oil
1 large onion or four shallots, finely chopped
1 cup (250 mL) beef stock or red wine
4 carrots, peeled and sliced in rounds
2 parsnips, peeled and cut into rounds
2 medium potatoes, peeled and cut into quarters

Sprinkle roast with salt and pepper. Rub with the flour and set aside. Heat oil in a heavy pot. Brown onion or shallots. Brown the roast well on all sides. Pour wine or stock around the roast and bring to a simmer. Cover and cook slowly. Turn the roast after half an hour. After one hour add the rest of the vegetables. Stir well and cook slowly with the lid on. Check that roast and vegetables are tender after one more hour. Cook longer if necessary. Place meat on a platter and circle with the vegetables. You can make a gravy with the pan juices or just skim the fat off and serve the pan juices in a warm jug. Serve with Horseradish Sauce. Serves 6-8.

Horseradish Sauce

1 cup (250 mL) sour cream
3 Tbsp. (45 mL) prepared horseradish

Mix well and refrigerate.

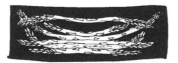

Going Potty

he term "herb garden" is loaded with evocative romantic appeal. It makes me think of monastic gardens laid out in beautifully symmetrical squares, or an Elizabethan garden in a manor house. I am dressed in appropriate costume and am gathering rose petals for potpourri and medications. The garden is full of the scent, flavor, and symbolism of herbs and flowers such as lilies (innocence and purity), bay trees (honor and triumph), and rosemary (fidelity in love).

Herbs can add great historical resonance and depth to our lives because we know they were used and enjoyed by the ancient Greeks and Romans and other peoples earlier in time. Not for me, you say. I live in a little apartment with a tiny balcony, or a townhouse with a mini-patio, or I rent a house and have an old garden full of shady shrubs and no sun.

I will not take no for an answer. I am here to convince you that you can have a little herb garden—and reap and harvest leaves and pleasure from these plants of many uses.

First you must think small and think pots. Luckily, today our nurseries and grocery stores have a wide selection of pots, from utilitarian to Italian terra cotta. Then look around your living space and see where you would place some herb pots. Look at balconies, windowsills, rooftops, skylights, front and back steps. Every living space has at least one place for a potted herb plant—unless you are living in a Neolithic cave (and there is still the cave entrance).

In fact the cave entrance, according to one garden historian, was probably the site of the first garden. Cave women who had discovered the plants in the forest they liked to harvest, dragged some to the cave and potted them up at the cave door. This was much safer and handier than wandering through the forest dodging saber-toothed tigers to gather edible plants and herbs.

Now that you have picked a few possible sites for your pots, it is time to trek off to the nursery and buy some pots and potting soil. If you are imaginative, you can create planters out of household items and spend very little on containers. Last summer, I made an Italian pot garden out of large, colorful olive oil tins. Often you can pick these up for a few dollars at Greek and Italian delis. Cut off the tops with tin snips and put some drainage holes in the bottom with a can punch. This collection of herbs planted in tins looked wonderful at the back door on a stone table. I planted basil, sage, oregano, Italian parsley, and rosemary. I have seen herbs planted in old boots, wooden boxes, battered buckets, old kettles, even old decaying rowboats. Go to the flea market or some garage sales and you will find cheap, unique receptacles for your plants.

Next—what to plant? As a former librarian I recommend that you go to the library and do a little research. Read some herb books and take note of the herbs you like the look of and want to plant. As most herbs are perennials or biennials, except dill and basil (which is perennial only in Maui and Mexico), plants are a good way to start. Seeding can be tricky for a beginner, and to guarantee you some success and immediate gratification (as Janis Joplin said, get it while you can), plants are the way to go. First-time gardeners should have some immediate success or they despair, become depressed, and vow never to attempt gardening again.

If you have favorite herbs you have tasted and loved, buy

those. Then branch out and expand your horizons. Here are my essential favorites. First basil, which appears in nurseries in the spring. It loves sun, rich soil, lots of water, and regular fertilizing (once a week). The plants also need some cover and protection at night for our coastal nights are too cold for this tropical plant. At the farm, our basil plants are put out in May in a plastic-covered tunnel with a little rotenone powder around them to stop the bugs with a basil habit.

By July, with luck the nights are warm enough and you can forgo tucking in your baby basils with their blanket. Snip off the blossoms as they appear or the plants will quit leaf production. Basil is the fussiest of all herbs to grow, but anything that tastes so rich and smells so fragrant is worth all the bother.

If you choose French tarragon, taste a leaf in the nursery when no one is looking. It should give your mouth a licorice hit and make your taste buds tingle. They could make a great toothpaste from tarragon. Russian tarragon, which looks almost exactly like its French cousin, has no flavor to speak of. It tastes of grass cuttings, in other words, lots of chlorophyll. Tarragon has a big root, so it needs a big pot, twelve inches (thirty centimetres) or more. It dies down and vacations from November to early March so don't fret and think you have killed it. Chives behave the same way. You cannot grow French tarragon by seed, only cuttings or root division. So you have to begin with a plant.

Rosemary loves being in a pot and makes a good houseplant in the winter. I have had a rosemary wreath in an Italian pot for six years. The pot has fat little round-bottomed cherubs dancing around the rim. I take it with me to lectures, TV spots, and classes. It is my herbal mascot. If you love the piny, peppery taste of this herb, buy several plants as it is a slow grower. A serious rosemary-loving cook can clear-cut one plant for a single recipe.

Rosemary loves a pinch of lime or wood ash and good drainage. Be careful not to dry it out in the pot. When it blooms it has heavenly blue flowers, which in myth bloomed when the Virgin Mary cast her cloak over a rosemary bush.

Pots of parsley make a neat row on a deck or patio. Little rows of herbs are always pleasing visually. They give a sense of order, and if your life is chaotic, gazing at your neat little pots will have a calming effect. Italian parsley has a more robust flavor and a flat leaf. They will sit out all winter barring the worst kind of cold snap.

Sage is happy in pots for several years. Then it will get too big and leggy and you should start anew. Mix red and silver for a decorative effect on your deck—and your turkey. It is easy to care for and delicious in pork dishes.

A pot of chives is a must for summer salads and don't be afraid to fling the blossoms in too. Once you have harvested the whole pot, fertilize and water and you should have a new crop in three weeks.

During the growing season herbs in pots need a weekly feed of either 20-20-20, fish fertilizer, or one of the new organic fertilizers on the market. I water daily and deadhead old blossoms and leaves. On my deck they flourish well into October when I bring in the bay and rosemarys to the house or the glassed-in front porch. Others I leave outside to winter over, such as chives, lemon thyme, sage, and sorrel. A west coast winter will not hurt them, but make sure they have drainage or the winter rains will rot out the roots. The basils I treat as annuals and dump for they start to wither in cool September nights.

An inspirational and utterly charming book is Abbie Zabar's *The Potted Herb*. Her advice and delightful drawings will encourage you to surround yourself with herbs in pots. Sarah Garland (who was fated to write about gardens) has written a pragmatic and beautiful book called *The Herb Garden*. To achieve pragmatic advice and beauty in the same book is a wonderful feat.

Herb plants are now available in most nurseries. Ten years ago it was very difficult to find more than chives and parsley, but the herbal revolution has happened. The best herb source by mail is Richters herb catalog (Goodwood, Ontario L0C 1A0). The catalog is a great learning source—good bathroom reading.

I envision your balcony now—crowded with pots of well-tended herbs. There is a deck chair and a small table, and you, my imagined urban dweller, are sitting with a glass of lemonade. Sprigs of your own mint are floating in the glass. You are peacefully waiting for your Cornish game hen to cook and it is stuffed with pieces of tarragon. In the refrigerator, some pale green, lemony sorrel soup is chilling.

The tending of plants has a healthy effect on people, and there is now serious study being made into so-called horticultural therapy. Plants can relieve depression, ease stress, and generally

brighten up your life. So fill your life with these life-enhancing plants. They will delight your taste buds, your nose, your eyes, and your fingers, as you touch and tend them. Chuck out that old drooping ficus tree. You cannot eat it. Go make yourself an herb garden instead.

Salmon with Sorrel Butter

This summertime recipe for salmon is adapted from Susan Belsinger and Carolyn Dille's book *Cooking with Herbs*.

2-lb. (900-g) piece of salmon fillet with skin on
1/4 cup (60 mL) melted butter (approx.)
1 shallot
1/3 cup (75 mL) dry white wine
1 1/2 cups (375 mL) finely chopped sorrel leaves
6 Tbsp. (90 mL) unsalted butter
Salt and pepper

Prepare a medium-hot charcoal fire. Brush the inside of the salmon with butter.

Mince the shallot and place in a heavy stainless steel or enameled saucepan with the wine and a little salt and pepper. Reduce the liquid to about 2 Tbsp. (30 mL).

In another stainless or enameled pan, wilt the sorrel for about 15 seconds. Remove the sorrel to a mortar and pound it with the unsalted butter.

Salt the salmon lightly and grill about 4 minutes on each side. As soon as the salmon is done, return the shallot and wine glaze to the stove and cook over low heat. Stir in the sorrel butter, cooking for about 30 seconds, just enough to heat it through. Season and remove from the heat.

Cut the salmon into 4 pieces. Reserve about 3 Tbsp. (45 mL) of the sorrel butter. Divide the rest among 4 warm serving plates and put a piece of lemon on each. Spoon the reserved butter over the salmon. Serves 4.

Rosemary Chicken

This is an Italian way of cooking chicken. The chicken turns golden brown and is redolent with rosemary. The same methods may be used for cooking a smaller frying chicken or for Cornish game hens. The recipe comes from my book *Summer Delights: Growing and Cooking Fresh Herbs*.

1 4-lb. (2-kg) roasting chicken
2 whole cloves garlic, peeled
2 whole cloves garlic, peeled and chopped
4 Tbsp. (60 mL) fresh rosemary leaves
Freshly ground black pepper (to taste)
1/4 cup (60 mL) olive or vegetable oil
1/4 cup (60 mL) dry white vermouth

Preheat oven to 375°F (190°C). Rinse chicken inside and out under cold running water and pat dry. Put chicken in a roasting pan. Place two whole garlic cloves, half the rosemary, and some pepper into the cavity of the chicken. Rub half of the oil on the skin of the chicken. Sprinkle chicken with chopped garlic, the remaining half of the rosemary, and pepper. Pour remaining half of oil in bottom of roasting pan, put roasting pan in oven, and bake for 1 1/2 hours, basting every 15 minutes.

When chicken is done, place it on a serving platter and return it to the oven to keep warm. Remove fat from roasting pan, scraping up pan juices. Use pan juices as a sauce. Carve chicken into slices. Pour sauce over top. Serve with pan-roasted potatoes and a green salad. Searves 4-6.

Puréed Summer Fruit with Lemon Balm

The first summer apples on our herb farm come from an ancient yellow transparent apple tree planted many years ago. The sheep stand under the tree waiting for them to fall. When the apples are ripe, the blackberries are ripe at the same time, making for an interesting coincidence. We cook apples and blackberries together with lemon balm. Lemon balm can also be added to applesauce. This recipe freezes well. Put a dollop of this summer fruit mixture on your morning cereal, or serve with ice cream. This recipe is included in *Summer Delights: Growing and Cooking Fresh Herbs*.

6-8 transparent apples, peeled, cored, and sliced
3-4 cups (750mL-1 L) ripe blackberries
1/4 cup (60 mL) sugar (optional)
1/4 cup (60 mL) chopped lemon balm
1 cup (250 mL) or less cold water

Mix apples, blackberries, sugar, lemon balm, and water together in a saucepan and bring to a boil. Reduce heat to low, cover and simmer for 10-15 minutes until fruit is cooked. Cool and serve, or chill in the refrigerator until ready to serve. Serves 4-6.

Rosemary Scones

This scone recipe is adapted from *Cooking with Herbs* by Susan Belsinger and Carolyn Dille.

2 cups (500 mL) whole wheat flour
2 cups (500 mL) unbleached white flour
1/2 tsp. (2 mL) salt
2 tsp. (10 mL) baking powder
1 tsp. (5 mL) baking soda
1 Tbsp. (15 mL) raw sugar
4 Tbsp. (60 mL) unsalted butter
2 Tbsp. (30 mL) finely chopped, fresh rosemary, or 2 tsp. (10 mL) dried rosemary, finely crumbled
1 1/2 cups (375 mL) buttermilk

In a large bowl, sift the flours, salt, baking powder, baking soda, and sugar. Cut the butter into the dry ingredients to make pea-sized lumps. Add the rosemary and buttermilk and mix together to form a soft dough.

Preheat oven to 400° (200°C).

Roll the dough out 1/2 inch (1 cm) thick on a lightly floured board. Cut into 1 1/2-inch (4-cm) squares and place close together on a greased and floured baking sheet. Bake for 20 minutes. Yields about 30 scones.

Enchanted April

Our south-facing slope has had its last frost, though in the valley below there are sometimes signs of frost and mist in the early morning. It is amazing that one can walk down the hill a quarter of a mile and find a different climate and a difference of several degrees in temperature. "April has come," we rejoice, happy that our winter hibernation is over.

The first Sunday afternoon in April always marks the opening of the farm for the spring and summer season of selling fresh-cut herbs and plants. Daffodils are blooming up both sides of the driveway, waving a cheery hello to visitors. The cherry trees are blooming with hazy pink arms reaching to the pale blue spring sky. The new lambs are full of courage and bounce and race up and down the rock hill playing king of the mountain. Sometimes they spring straight up in the air and then butt each other. They rush to their mum and bang her milk bag to make the milk flow. If she has just fed them, she moves on and they give up for a short time and rush off to play. Joker the donkey has to be put in a separate field as the lambs make him jealous and nasty and he kicks out at them with his hind legs. He is like an angry three-year-old sibling who wishes the new baby had not been born. Balefully he stares through the fence at the cavorting lambs and I give him extra carrots to soothe him.

Tables are put out in front of the barn where we place the new plants for sale. It is early days yet but there are tarragon, chives, and oregano ready to pop into someone's garden. People ask for basil with longing in their voices, but it is too early to put basil out (a tender tropical). At this time of year, one can start basil in the house so by May it can be put out under plastic. Lots of dusting and tidying to do as we drag out stuff from the barn where it has sat all winter. Laura and Morris our caretakers ready the little cottage for her soap and craft sales. With straw on the floor, baskets hanging from the ceiling, and the shelves filled with glowing jellies and stacks of homemade soap, Laura has created a little bit of country theater and fantasy for customers. Last winter she went down the road to the local school and taught children how to make soap and patchwork quilts. Old-fashioned country crafts are still alive and well.

If it rains the first Sunday we are open, we move the tables and plants into the barn and it is cozy listening to the rain beat on the tin roof and watching the peacocks find safe roosting places up in the beams. They have not been disturbed all winter and now they get a little flustered when they see people drive into *their* field and walk into *their* barn. Twelve o'clock comes and cars start up the driveway. It is wonderful to see old friends and customers after the winter. Children have grown, gardens have changed. People move and lose their treasured herb plots and have to start new ones, and so they come with lists and designs on paper.

We have taken the overwintering plants out of the greenhouse and washed and tidied them up for opening day. Some of the bay trees have scale, but when the leaves are washed and the brown ones picked off and a little compost given to them they perk up and begin to flourish. Being out in the cool spring air seems to drive off the bugs. There are some deaths and one must be ruthless and hurl them out, although I once threw out a bay that had died back to the roots after a heavy frost. It sat discarded on the edge of the burn pile for a few weeks and one day I noticed little green tips pushing through. I quickly rescued it and put it in a fat Italian terra cotta pot, where it has happily been living, green and bushy, for the past five years.

The spring light is startling this time of year. Not the raucous blaze of summer but a clear clean silver filtered light that is softer and suits spring bulbs. When the daffodils are done, the bluebells appear and under a small grove of Douglas firs there is a solid thatch of bluebells that spreads every year and survives people and dogs walking through it. The lungwort (an old medicinal herb) is blooming and has lovely blue flowers that mix well with the tulips. We always end up digging roots of it up for customers who want what is blooming in the garden now. I doubt if it is used to cure lung diseases these days, but many ancient herbs have a place in the garden for their beauty, color, or historical connections, which link us to our ancestors past.

In the vegetable garden in mid-April the asparagus arrives and we eat it every night for a month and I do not feel surfeited. I cook it very quickly in the steamer for only a couple of minutes and give it a flick of butter, lemon juice, and ground pepper. It is delicious cold the next day in a salad. I remember asparagus sandwiches in my childhood made especially for Father's bridge club. When the meeting was over I would secretly eat the leftover ones with great pleasure. The soft white crustless bread, the tart mayonnaise, and the crunch of the round green asparagus stalk remains a powerful taste memory.

We are just finishing the Belgian endive about this time. I take a sharp knife and bury my hand in the sawdust where it has been hiding all winter to retrieve the last ones. Raw, steamed, or baked, this tart piquant vegetable can be a whole meal, especially when wrapped in a thin piece of ham and spread with rich bay-flavored béchamel sauce. This is often my favorite Easter lunch with a crusty loaf and a bottle of Hainle Vineyards Baco Noir, which Shari Darling in her useful *Canada's Cheese and Wine Lovers' Cookbook* recommends. When Easter comes I get out my egg collection. Eggs are the perfect round symbol of rebirth, fertility, and spring. My sister in Alberta sends me Ukrainian decorated eggs, which I treasure. They look handsome on the dark oak table with small bouquets of daffodils. German poet Rainer Maria Rilke sums up the new season perfectly.

> *Spring has returned.*
> *The earth is like a child*
> *that knows poems.*

Get a Head Start with Basil

Serious pesto lovers who want to grow their own basil need a small cold frame or plastic tunnel to ensure a long harvesting period for this subtropical herb.

Start the seeds indoors from late March until June or buy young plants to set out under plastic in spring or early summer. July plantings are normally fine without protection.

Sow two seeds, 1/8 inch (3 mm) deep in each 1 1/2-inch-wide (4-cm) plastic or fiber pot or soil block. Use a soilless dampened potting mix. Cover the trays of containers with clear plastic to retain moisture. A temperature of 75° to 80°F (23° to 26°C) is necessary for germination within four days, so place your tray over a heating unit. When the first leaves appear, the plastic cover should be removed and the tray placed in a bright window. The seedlings will need a feed of half-strength liquid fish fertilizer every week. Weed or transplant extra seedlings so you have one to each container. Our seedlings are grown in a high-windowed room that reaches 75°F (23°C) in the day and 55° to 60°F (12° to 15°C) at night; they do not seem to suffer transplanting shock when planted out in a cold frame.

At 3 or 4 inches (7.5 or 10 cm) in height, the seedlings are ready to be transplanted to a cold frame or plastic tunnel or to an 8-inch-wide (20-cm) pot for indoor or patio growth. The soil should be fertile and high in organic material and should also drain quickly. Aphids can be controlled with a weak detergent and water spray or by thumb and forefinger.

Harvest starts in late June or July by cutting off each growth point and the next set of leaves. Harvesting can be every week for a light cut or every other week for a heavy cut.

—Andrew Yeoman

Asparagus

here are many wonderful things that one could dream of inheriting: a stately home, a Picasso, a silver spoon in one's mouth. But I think a delightful thing to inherit is an asparagus patch. When we bought our farm fourteen years ago, there was an established asparagus bed. The lady who had planted it had moved next door, and for the next several years I took her some asparagus as a form of tithing-thanks for her original work.

I grew up with an asparagus bed, which was my father's great love. He tended and nurtured it with obsessive care. The first spears of spring were brought to the kitchen with much reverence and ceremony. If there were only a few, he ate them all! This was my first realization that patriarchy existed—but I quickly learned to sneak one or two spears and eat them raw in the garden when no one was looking. Ah, the heavenly green crunch—that new pea flavor.

I remember my first meal in France. I had just spent three months living in the south of Spain with my two young daughters. It was May and we drove over the French border past Deauville and pulled into a tiny seaside village late in the afternoon. We asked a lady on the road where we could find a bed and *bonne cuisine* and she directed us to a small inn near the beach. Four large freight trucks were parked outside, and luckily there was one room left with two large feather beds. We came down for dinner.

Grandmother was in the bar, all in black, watching TV, knitting, and casting an eye over everything that went on. We sat down to dinner with the truck drivers and our first course quickly arrived. It was a huge white platter filled with white spears of asparagus, each one as thick as the truckers' thumbs and incredibly tender. They were served simply with some melted butter. The rest of the meal has faded from memory, but I will never forget that platter of gleaming white asparagus. The beauty and simplicity of the dish was utter perfection.

James Beard said asparagus was the greatest gift of the old world to the new. It reached North America in the seventeenth century and was brought by the early English settlers in Virginia. It was originally native to Eastern and Central Europe. The word asparagus came from an ancient Persian-Greek word *asparagos,* meaning "to sprout." In Latin, the word became *sperage,* and in eighteenth-century England it was called sparrowgrass. It was used as a medicine, probably as a spring tonic before it was firmly established as a vegetable. It can act as a diuretic, is low in calories, and contains vitamins A and C plus potassium and phosphorus.

Probably because of its phallic shape, asparagus has long been considered an aphrodisiac and was fed continuously to timid bridegrooms in France. *Culpepper's Herbal* has a recipe that is a decoction of asparagus roots boiled in wine. He suggests you take it while fasting for several mornings and "it will stirreth up bodily lust in man and woman."

Louis the XIV had forcing beds in his vegetable gardens at Versailles so he could eat asparagus in January. In the nineteenth century, Britain grew more asparagus than any country in Europe. London was ringed by asparagus farms. So this soft, voluptuous vegetable has been the favorite of gourmands and royalty for centuries. In Europe, it is nearly always blanketed with straw and the spear never sees the sun. White asparagus is much preferred and probably has less vitamin value because it is not green. In North America, we seem to prefer the green.

Cooks in Europe usually peel the spears up to the tip, which ensures tenderness and means more of the tough stalk may be eaten. I never peel our asparagus because it is always exquisitely tender. Much-traveled asparagus from a market would probably benefit from peeling.

The asparagus season is April through the middle of June. After that you should stop picking so the plant can build up its strength for next year. The delicate fronds appear and decorate your garden or bouquet until November, when they turn yellow. We clip ours down, give the bed a good feed of rotted manure, and the asparagus sleeps until spring. It pokes its first spears up in April or May when the soil has warmed up, giving it the right encouragement to rise out of bed.

When buying asparagus, choose fat spears that are tightly closed. Keep them cool and damp by wrapping them in a wet tea towel and storing in the refrigerator or, as Julia Child suggests, put them in a container upright with two inches (five centimetres) of water around the butts. Cover with a loose plastic bag and refrigerate. They will keep this way for two to three days.

There are many methods of cooking asparagus and various schools of thought. I barely cook my just-picked spears for two to three minutes in a large, flat, stainless steel frying pan. Sometimes I steam them in a bamboo steamer or sauté them quickly in a stir-fry. Store-bought asparagus can take longer to cook because it is tougher. I like it still bright green with crunch. Drain quickly and serve with some butter, a grind of pepper, and a squeeze of lemon. I love the look of asparagus on the deep green pottery plates I lugged home from Provence a few years ago. The two shades of green are a welcome visual message of spring and renewal. Through May and June we eat asparagus every night and we never tire of it. Occasionally, I put it in a quiche or serve it cold and marinated in a salad, but plain with butter is my preference.

The culinary world has created asparagus steamers so you can cook it standing up and just steam the tips. There are also many accoutrements such as asparagus tongs, forks, and ceramic plates decorated with asparagus designs with which to grace your table. I am most happy, however, eating asparagus with my fingers, and having read that Queen Victoria and many aristocratic duchesses did the same, I am quite content and free of guilt over stuffy table manners. Large napkins and finger bowls serve to fix the buttery-fingers problem.

Asparagus pairs well with roast chicken stuffed with lemon balm and basted with lemon juice, vermouth, and a touch of olive oil. Served with new potatoes, this is the perfect spring dinner for special friends. I still cannot pass the asparagus bed without snitching a few spears and remembering my father, who nourished my passion for asparagus, an enduring source of pleasure even fifty years later.

Rebecca's Asparagus Sandwich

Rebecca is an old foodie friend and a chef in her own restaurant in Victoria. Her unique California flair is evident in this sandwich.

8-12 spears of fresh asparagus
1/4 cup (60 mL) soy sauce
2 Tbsp. (30 mL) sesame oil
1 tsp. (5 mL) Vietnamese chili paste or 1/4 tsp. (1 mL) chili flakes
4 thin to medium slices of mozzarella
4 slices crusty French or Italian bread
1/4 cup (60 mL) toasted almonds
Butter

Wash and pat dry asparagus. Mix soy sauce, sesame oil, and chili paste in a frying pan. Heat and stir well. Sauté the washed asparagus in this marinade for 1-2 minutes. Place the mozzarella cheese on both slices of bread and sprinkle the toasted almonds on the cheese. Lay the cooked asparagus on one side of the sandwich. Close the sandwich and butter the top slice of bread. Place 2 Tbsp. (30 mL) of butter in a frying pan and cook the sandwich until golden brown on both sides and the cheese has melted. Cut on a diagonal and place on a plate with one half standing up straight to show the beautiful interior. Makes 2 sandwiches.

Asparagus Japanese-style

2 lbs. (900 g) fresh asparagus
3 Tbsp. (45 mL) vegetable oil
3 Tbsp. (45 mL) toasted sesame seeds
4 Tbsp. (60 mL) vinegar
4 Tbsp. (60 mL) sugar
1 Tbsp. (15 mL) soy sauce
Salt to taste

Steam the asparagus 2-3 minutes until tender and crisp. Drain asparagus, cool in cold water, and drain. Heat oil and sesame seeds in a pan until seeds are golden. Set aside and cool. Add vinegar, sugar, soy sauce, and salt and mix well. Cut asparagus slantwise into pieces. Pour sauce over asparagus and stir so all pieces are covered. Chill and serve. Serves 4-6.

A Goddess Makes Bread

n May of 1991, I had a religious experience. The International Association of Culinary Professionals, a large organization of chefs, cookbook writers, cooking teachers, and restaurant owners, had met in Vancouver that spring for a week-long conference. Julia Child had been declared Scholar-in-Residence, so it was with great excitement that I signed up for her one cooking class—a bread-baking session. The chance to see the Queen of Cuisine in action and not just on television was obviously very enticing because that morning about 200 people gathered in a large room with a raised dais to watch Julia perform.

I suppose I can blame my English professors of long ago for teaching me to look for metaphors; in fact it has become a slight obsession with me. I like to make connections and comparisons and link parts of my life together. As I sat among this group of women, I noticed a palpable state of fervency in the air. Each member of the crowd was holding her body in a slightly forward position and was gazing at the dais where Julia was to appear.

Then I noticed many of the women were holding dark-blue hardcover books—many of which were tattered and shabby. They were clutching these books as if they were missals or prayerbooks. A closer look revealed them to be copies of Julia's first book, *Mastering the Art of French Cooking,* which was first published in the early sixties when Julia appeared on television from Boston and began to create her following of devoted cooks, forever changing the menus of dinner parties all across North America in the process.

Her friend of forty years had come along as Julia's baking companion. Rosemary was as tall as Julia with white hair pulled into an elegant bun. Also on the stage were numerous stoves and worktables and a clutch of assistants—young Vancouver cooking fans crisply dressed in white shirts and aprons. They stood in the background waiting for orders from Julia.

Of course to do a bread class in a short time, many yeast mixtures have to be started earlier. Julia and Rosemary began to stir and mix and my metaphor machine began to whir. Of course, I thought, this is an altar. Julia and Rosemary are the great goddesses, and the young women in aprons are the attendants or acolytes. The mixing continued, and then the kneading began. The audience listened very carefully to the Goddess's words and many wrote them down in the backs of their tattered prayerbooks. Many kinds of loaves were made: white baguettes, whole wheat, sandwich loaves, focaccia, and rolls.

The sense of fervency heightened and suddenly my breath caught in my chest. A slight error had been made! Julia recognized she had made focaccia with whole wheat dough. She uttered a goddess-like pronouncement with a twinkle in her eye. "Now whole wheat focaccia is trendy," she said in her sonorous voice, and the congregation nodded in agreement for no one argues with the Goddess.

The room soon began to fill with the heavenly incense of bread baking. The tension was increasing for the miracle of making bread was soon to reach its high point in this great life-affirming ceremony. The bread was pulled from the oven, and a soft "oooh" sound filled the room. The bread was then sliced into small, communion-wafer-sized pieces and placed in large baskets.

The acolytes stepped down from the altar and passed the baskets of bread to the communicants. The warm pieces of life-giving bread were eaten with a slow reverent chewing. I expected to hear a heavenly choir sing, but there was only silence.

Then the Goddess Julia stepped down from the altar and joined the throng. Women worshippers crowded around her, pushing their tattered books towards her with pens so she could place her mark upon them.

Finally, books signed, the congregation left the hall. The altar stoves were turned off and the acolytes cleaned the dais of dishes and remaining dough. Julia and her friend Rosemary left the hallowed place and we were, all of us, happy and serene to have seen the Goddess in the flesh and to have shared with her in the amazing and life-affirming act of making and eating our daily bread together as if in communion service.

Older women are seldom revered in our Western society and it pleases me to see Julia Child given respect and adulation. She appears on television and has a huge following and yet she is not young, skinny, and sexually provocative—the usual requirements for television exposure. Her zest for life, cooking, and eating permeate her books and television shows and public appearances. She is a truly wonderful role model and, of course, this is exactly what goddesses should be—examples for us all.

Basic French Bread

This recipe uses techniques from Julia Child's French bread recipe from *Mastering the Art of French Cooking.* Julia's recipe is many pages long and many, many steps. This version is simpler for mere mortals.

You can set this bread to rise, go off for several hours, and then come home and finish it. Often I set it to rise in the morning and bake it right before dinner. The secret to leaving the bread is to let it rise in a cool place, about 65°F (18°C). The longer the rise, the better the bread. Recipe makes 2 loaves.

1/2 cup (125 mL) warm water
1 tsp. (5 mL) sugar
1/4 tsp. (1 mL) powdered ginger (this is a yeast improver)
2 Tbsp. (30 mL) dry yeast
5 cups (1.25 L) unbleached white flour
2 cups (500 mL) warm water
2 Tbsp. (30 mL) sugar
1 1/2 tsp. (7 mL) salt
2 Tbsp. (30 mL) olive oil
1/4 cup (60 mL) finely chopped sage, rosemary, or a herb of choice
(optional)
1 cup (250 mL) flour
1 egg beaten
1 Tbsp. (15 mL) water
Chopped herbs for garnish

Combine the water, 1 tsp. (5 mL) sugar, ginger, and yeast in a bowl and let stand about 10 minutes.

Place the 5 cups (1.25 L) of flour in a large mixing bowl and make a well in the middle of the flour. Place the two cups (500 mL) of warm water, the bubbling yeast mixture, and the 2 Tbsp. (30 mL) of sugar in the depression. Mix enough flour into the yeast mixture to slightly thicken it. Let stand for about 20 minutes. The yeast mixture will mound up and bubble in the center. Add the salt and oil and stir the rest of the flour into the bowl. If you are adding the optional herbs to the inside of the bread, add them with the oil and salt. Mix well with a wooden spoon; the dough will be stiff.

Put the last cup (250 mL) of flour on a smooth surface and turn out the dough. Knead firmly and with energy for 10 minutes. Set the timer so you do not cheat. When done, the dough should form a smooth, non-sticky ball. Lightly oil the bowl and the dough and replace the dough in the bowl. Cover with a clean cloth and let rise for at least 2 hours, until doubled in size.

Punch down, let rise again for another hour until doubled. Punch and roll into round or long tapered loaves. Place on cookie sheets that have been sprinkled with cornmeal. Let rise until almost doubled, about forty minutes.

Preheat oven to 450°F (230°C). To make a good crust, place a pan of water in the bottom of the oven. Beat the egg with 1 Tbsp. (15 mL) water and brush the loaves with the egg wash. Using a sharp knife, make slashes across each loaf at an angle. Sprinkle the loaves with chopped rosemary, sage, or other herbs. Place the bread immediately in the hot oven.

Within the first three minutes, spray water into the oven (a few squirts from a plant sprayer will do). Bake for about 40-45 minutes. If it is getting too brown, lower the heat to 350°F (180°C). When the bread is done, place on racks to cool. This bread freezes well. To serve, wrap in foil and heat for 20 minutes at 400°F (200°C).

Living from
Land to Mouth

May is an incredibly busy month in the garden. Andrew the gardener can hardly be enticed to leave the farm, so engrossed is he in planting vegetables for eating this summer and of course next winter.

Early in May, garden gamblers can sneak in a row of bush beans and corn. There is a chance that the weather will be too cold and damp and the seeds will rot, but if the weather is warm and balmy you will have early beans and corn. Andrew starts his early seeds in soil blocks in the house and sets them out as young plants. This gamble is reasonably safe; all you have to lose are some seeds—not the family fortune.

In May, the main crop potatoes are planted ('Pontiacs' or 'Yukon Golds'). Often at this time of year one can scavenge for some volunteer new potatoes that missed being harvested last fall. They are lovely surprises, small and tender—a free gift for dinner and a treat after winter-stored red potatoes that are getting a little sprouty. The volunteer dill appears this time of year as well, and I love this garden synchronicity. An old prairie gardener friend once told me that when the dill came up she knew the soil was warm enough for her seeds to germinate. A signal from nature to plant.

Andrew is a great believer in protection from wind chill for his new seedlings. Basil plants are under a plastic row tunnel supported by white curved irrigation pipe cut in lengths to support the plastic.

Pepper plants and eggplants, which are heat-loving, are in a cold frame. There are various pieces of cold frame sections that can be moved about like pieces of Lego. As the plants get taller, more pieces can be added. The tomatoes are in a raised bed walled with plastic, with no roof. This cuts the wind and warms up the soil. 'Oregon Spring', 'Early Cherry', 'Celebrity', and 'Golden Delight' are our favorites. This protection gives us ripe tomatoes at the end of July.

The corn is planted inside a cold frame box for an early start. 'Peaches and Cream' and 'Sugar Dots' are our choice and we can usually pick in the first week in August. The cucumbers and squash are put in as seeds, or often as small plants from the nursery. Dill and cilantro are seeded. Cilantro, which goes to seed so quickly (when your back is turned), should be sown every couple of weeks. One sowing will not last the summer. Because it does go to seed quickly, though, often one gets a volunteer crop in the early fall. Carrots are sown from seed and covered with Reemay cloth to prevent the pesky carrot fly. Continue planting lettuces and arugula. Some that was self-sown are already up. Besides salad, I put the spicy arugula leaves in soups and pasta sauces. Summer peas are sown and a disease-resistant variety such as sugar snap 'Snappy' is a good choice. It grows to a height of five feet (150 centimetres).

Of course, with all this flurry of planting one mustn't forget to raise one's head from the garden occasionally in May to observe the intense green of spring and of course to check on what is edible now!

The artichokes, for example, are ready to harvest. You are actually eating the blossom of this large silvery plant. It is perfect for the back of a large flower bed for it is beautiful *and* practical, not just a bimbo in the garden patch. Artichokes winter over well in a coastal garden except when there is an extreme cold snap.

The first artichoke dinner is an annual treat. If you pick them quite small there is no fuzzy choke and you can eat virtually the whole heart. The artichoke, dipped in melted butter with fresh lemon squeezed on it, is one of my favorite vegetables, though one brother-in-law, on eating them for the first time, said it was like eating "goddam pinecones."

Other things are growing on the farm besides seeds. Wild baby rabbits are multiplying in the Brer Rabbit blackberry patch below the pool. They get bold because they seem to know that the ancient farm cat only has four teeth left and her hunting days have waned. The dogs chase their scent, but they scurry back into their haven of blackberries homefree.

The compost bins have been emptied on the garden beds, the black treasure spread carefully over the soil. New compost is being made and the bins are filling up again with grass cuttings, sheep manure, and all the house compostables.

The French sorrel is lush and green. This is a very reliable perennial herb for the cook. I like to make Spring Tonic Sorrel Soup in May. It is such a fresh green lemony-tasting soup that it perks up the palate as a first course. It looks very pretty with chive flowers sprinkled across or a few pink shrimps as a garnish, the shrimp looking as if they are swimming on a pale green sea.

The apple, pear, and plum trees are blooming, the meadows are newly green, the rosemary bushes are sporting pale blue flowers. I have read stories of the south of France where women fling their clean sheets over the rosemary bushes and at night your bed is scented with the cold, sharp, piny smell. Much more romantic than an electric dryer and the chemical scent of dryer sheets.

I rearrange my pots on the patio and plant daisies, herbs, and silver dusty miller. I have collected pots for years and I like the decisions I have to make every season—what will go in this pot? Some of the Italian pots are attaining an amazing patina of age, moss, and water stains. They look as if they came from an old Italian villa. I drag out my giant cymbidium orchid, which is blooming. It sits outside from May until October, happy to be in our temperate climate. When it gets too big we chop it in pieces and give parts to friends.

I like creeping prostrate rosemary in clay pots because it droops and hangs over the pot in a charming way. I also have little myrtles, like mini trees, in pots. It is an endlessly entertaining hobby: the search for the right pot, the perfect plant. And you can clip them, tend them, shuffle and rearrange them daily.

Pots on the patio can lead one into that dangerous and expensive pursuit "nursery cruising." I hear the sensible gardener's voice saying, "Don't buy unless you have a place for it." We belong to two different schools of thought, he to "less is more," and me to "less is bore." In a four-mile radius of the farm there are five excellent nurseries to lead me into temptation. But there are worse addictions, I say: "It could be gin!"

May is wisteria month. The pale pendulous mauve flowers drip from the pergola roof and the scent makes one delirious. Why is there no perfume called wisteria? The blossoms all fall on the patio at the end of May and I sweep up the pale mauve flowers and then the green leaves appear. Our wisteria was planted about 1912 when our old farmhouse was built. It is a noble old vine and has withstood the renovations and changes to the old house over the past eighty-five years. It has developed thick twisting vines where the robins nest in the summer.

Just beyond our farm new things are happening and happily they are rural, agricultural happenings. Three small vineyards have been planted in the past two years. Perhaps this will be Napa Valley North in a decade or so. Part of the valley has been planted in daffodils, an amazing sight when they are blooming. And one of the oldest pioneer homesites across the valley was designated as a Heritage Farm site. The first log cabin was built in 1858 when a Scottish family called Lidgate settled there and began to farm. There have been seven generations of the family since then and the last four attended the ceremony. The farm still exists with rolling meadows and a pond. Luckily it has not been urbanized. It is good to see some historical and agricultural continuity in this beautiful small valley.

We need to treasure and care for our agricultural heritage and remember the first pioneer farms and farmers. The land needs to be preserved so we can grow our food near to where it will be consumed. On this note I will make a May salad of the first spring lettuces for lunch and savor each leaf. This is truly living from land to mouth.

Spring Tonic Sorrel Soup

Serve this soup cold or warm, depending on the weather. It is a refreshing
way to start a dinner party.

4 cups (1 L) washed sorrel leaves, stems removed
4 shallots, finely chopped
4 Tbsp. (60 mL) butter
2 cups (500 mL) chicken stock
1 1/2 cups (375 mL) half-and-half cream or milk
Freshly ground pepper
Chopped chives, chive flowers or some cooked, shelled shrimp

Cook sorrel leaves in a saucepan with very little water until limp. Drain and
purée in a blender or food processor. Set aside.

Sauté shallots in butter for 3 or 4 minutes. Add chicken stock and
bring to a boil. Reduce heat and simmer for 5 minutes. Add puréed sorrel to
stock and whisk together until smooth. Add cream to mixture and blend in.
Season with pepper. Serve hot or cold and garnish with chopped chives,
chive flowers, and/or cooked shrimp. Serves 2-4

Spring Vinaigrette for First Lettuces

In a jar with a lid, place 1/4 cup (60 mL) rice wine vinegar, 3/4 cup
(175 mL) of olive oil, some fresh ground black pepper, 1 Tbsp. (15 mL)
Dijon mustard and 4 Tbsp. (60 mL) chopped chives. Shake well.

Serve over freshly picked garden lettuce. Use sparingly or you will
swamp the delicate flavor of the lettuce. Refrigerate the remaining
vinaigrette. It will keep for a week. Your own home dressing is so easy and
quick to make that you never need to buy bottled dressing again.

June is Busting Out All Over

June is the lushest of all months of the year. It truly busts out all over just as the Rodgers and Hammerstein song says it does. All the maples and alders have leafed out, and the three huge copper beeches that grace and dominate the garden are also out in their full red-bronze glory. The small rose garden of old roses is in full flourish and I try to keep up with the dead-heading and watering. The old roses seem hardier and less prone to bugs and the dreaded black spot. When it appears I take off my glasses and squint and the spots disappear in a Monet-myopic fuzziness that is very pleasing.

In fact, one cannot look at the garden at its zenith without thinking of Monet. Once while in France, Andrew and I took the train from Paris to see the famous Impressionist's garden in Giverny. We walked three miles from the station through the countryside, snooping in all the gardens along the way. There were statuesque artichoke plants, and neat rows of lettuce and peas. One could imagine the menus for the evening dinner by observing the gardens. Giverny, newly restored by vast amounts of American foundation money, was a delight. The bridges over the ponds, the lilies, the nasturtiums crawling down the gravel paths: all were perfect. Best of all was the kitchen with its famous gay yellow plates and Japanese prints on the walls. The Monet family cared much about dinner and have left recipes and a domestic history behind for us to study. I am sure the yellow hits of color in my kitchen (the sink and many bowls of all sizes), are there because of my visit that afternoon.

The peonies are out in the vegetable garden. To some they are a strange combination, but they stand as sentinels at the end of the long raised beds. Their huge shaggy pink, white, and crimson heads bow under the weight of their showy petals.

The full harvesting of summer vegetable crops has not yet begun but there are fresh peas, lettuces, artichokes, and best of all strawberries. We eat strawberries for breakfast, lunch, and dinner and if I overdo it I break out in large hives. Andrew makes strawberry jam and hoards it in a dark cupboard for winter. I like to look at it lined up on the counter waiting for him to label with his calligraphy pen.

The dogs have also discovered the joys of berries and snuffle down the rows munching happily. They also surf down the lines of raspberry canes in early July eating with a rare delicacy, cleaning out all the berries at dog level. There is a certain bearlike quality to their berry-picking behavior. It is all right though because, frankly, I do not want to bend to that level to pick.

The four lambs are getting big and losing their adorable cuteness. Their faces now look a little piggy. They go to market at the end of June and at this time of year I feel that age-old ambivalence and my vegetarian feelings run high. The day they are picked up the mothers *baa* in a sad, desolate way and I usually withdraw from the farm so as to miss the leavetaking.

June is a traditional month for much happier occasions— weddings—and indeed it was on the summer solstice that my youngest daughter, Jenny, married her English boyfriend, David, in the garden. The barn was decorated with boughs, greenery, and flowers for a dance, and the peacocks flew to the rafters to observe the strange carryings-on. The much-discussed menu included barbecued salmon and of course strawberries. For months before we were all hoping desperately for a wonderful mid-summer's eve with clear skies and no rain. If it did rain, we would use plan B and decamp to the newly cleaned and bedecked barn and listen to the rain on the tin roof. But it did not rain, and the day, sunny and warm, was all we could have hoped for.

Walking the Mt. Newton Valley road is a favorite pastime of mine in June. In some stretches, the oaks curve over to form a leafy tunnel of green, and the Queen Anne's lace and wild blue chicory dot the sides of the road. A mile from the farm, lower down in the valley, is a tiny white clapboard church called St. Stephen's. The church, which was designated a heritage building last summer, was built by the first Scottish and English pioneers in 1864.

The old graves are sheltered with long wisps of dripping silver Spanish moss that give the place a misty Gothic touch. Prowling among them I find the gravestone of Walter Thomson, who built our farmhouse in 1910 and planted many of the trees we treasure today. I say thank you to Walter. I walk home past the huge medieval-style barn that squats prominently in the valley offering shelter to the cattle, the hay crop, and the swallows.

So June passes. The green lushness gives this month an intensity that changes with the dry heat of July. In the evening, just before dark, I sit on the patio and watch the swallows swoop over the pool for their last drink or insect before darkness falls. We go to bed knowing we will hear the cry of Alex the peacock as dawn breaks and knowing also that we will have strawberries again for breakfast.

Arugula

(also called rocket or rucola)

Sowing arugula seed in June, if done in the open, produces hot-flavored and slightly stringy leaves that will soon be peppered with holes from the attention of the flea beetle. Sowing in June, if done under a floating row cover, such as Reemay, produces succulent, tender, nutty-flavored greens that will give an uplifting spiciness to any salad.

The floating row cover acts like a mini-greenhouse, allowing the passage of air and moisture but retaining high humidity around the plant in dry weather.

Arugula survives neglect and poor soil, but it is at its best with rich soil and watering every other day in dry periods. I like to sow seeds thickly and start harvesting thinnings when the plants are only 3 to 4 inches (7.5 to 10 cm) high. Some seedlings are left 4 to 6 inches (10 to 15 cm) apart to mature into larger plants for later harvesting. Arugula is an ideal container plant as it can be sown thickly and harvested when young like a giant sproutling.

Arugula seeds are available from Territorial Seeds and Richters. Reemay or an equivalent floating row cover is carried by many garden centers.

—Andrew Yeoman

The Swallows of Summer

he hammock is strung between a copper beech and a giant cedar and if you fall out you land in thick ivy. The pool is clean and swimmable for the battle of the algae has been won. The dogs love to drop their red rubber ball in the pool and watch someone else rescue it.

We have a small rubber raft that we blow up and float in the pool. To lie on this with a glass of wine and a book is one of those perfect summer things to do. It has a *Swallows and Amazons* feel to it—though you are only a few feet from shore, you feel free from adult restraints.

I did not read *Swallows and Amazons* until I was an adult and it was love at first read. Susan, the book's heroine, took a cookbook along on her adventures and made it her responsibility to look after supplies and to feed everyone. This I could identify with, not because of altruism but because of the salutary fact that: the one who looks after the supplies and the cooking is the one guaranteed to get food. Two things make me feel very insecure: a poorly stocked refrigerator and a shortage of books to read.

July and August have a rhythm on the farm that is marked by the ripening of fruits and vegetables. Raspberries come on in early July and I make lots of freezer jam. I have to make it as soon as I have picked the berries. Raspberries do not wait and they decay more quickly than any fruit I can think of. Ravenhill raspberry jam (recipe straight off the Certo bottle) has the freshest, fruitiest, jammiest taste, and a certain nephew-in-law who gets a jar now and then says it's better than sex. Andrew makes cooked raspberry jam and likes it better. The color is a darker red and it tastes sweeter and more like old-fashioned jam. So the great raspberry jam debate continues and we each have our own jars at breakfast.

New potatoes are being dug. I love them cold the next day, straight from the fridge with a sprinkle of salt. They make a lovely salad for lunch with chopped tarragon or chives, pepper, and a little green olive oil.

Green peas are picked in July (ours seldom make it to the pot) and are usually used as an appetizer. To sit on the patio in the late afternoon, shelling and eating peas and sipping wine and chatting with a friend—all in a desultory fashion—is a perfect summer pastime. The dogs covet the pea pods and abscond with them under the table to munch them happily in the shade.

The first zucchinis appear and we try to pick them young and small. Sometimes they hide amongst the leaves and an enormous green blimp appears. Here the chickens get lucky. I slice up the dirigible and take it to the henhouse. We have added a bantam rooster to the farmyard. He is cream and golden brown (a Buff Brahma) and has three matching golden wives. Despite his small stature he does not lack confidence and he leads the attack on the zucchini slices, disregarding the hens who are twice his size. The Buff ladies lay tiny, pale, cream-colored eggs, which are a delight to gather, look at, and eat—two bites and the egg is gone.

Early August there is first corn and then tomatoes. They come early as they have been in plastic cold frames with no tops. This gives them the extra warmth needed to hurry up the ripening. Years ago during my Alberta sojourn, I learned what to do with green tomatoes but now I revel in ripe ones. I ignore the store tomatoes all winter so that the summer crop is an excuse for a feast, and we eat them twice a day. I like them for breakfast on hot buttered toast with a swish of cream cheese and a basil leaf chopped on top.

The herb crop is at its peak and I scout through my cookbooks to find new ways to use my wealth of basil. Sometimes I sit on the edge of the garden and pop a hot tomato in my mouth and follow it with a basil leaf chaser—who needs to cook? We sell bags and bags on Sundays when the farm is open. People drive up the driveway with the glazed look in their eyes of the serious basil addict. They have to come early for often by three o'clock there is none left and sometimes they beg—knowing no shame.

The rhythm of the ripening continues and the corn appears. If we have lots of people for dinner we can dash down the road to Silver Rill Farm and buy beautiful corn and rush back to cook it. I have heard of raccoons stealing corn and farmers putting transistor radios playing rock music in the corn patch. We have raccoons who lust over the chickens and the baby geese, but luckily they have not found the corn patch.

The peach tree is espaliered against the kitchen wall and from the sink you can see ripe peaches hanging—waiting to be picked. A just-picked peach is a lovely start to the day, especially if someone peels and slices it for you and puts it in your favorite yellow bowl.

The prolific yellow plums ripen, and the yellow transparent apples are ready in the sheep pasture. I share them with the sheep: One for me and two for the sheep. Transparents mush and bruise quickly if dropped so the sheep hang about and watch the picker very closely.

Blackberries are another staple of a B.C. summer. There are two large patches on the farm and the picking is easy. We make pies, jam, jelly, vinegar, and, best of all, blackberry sorbet. It has such an intense summer flavor and is such a deep purple that a few scoops of this sorbet decorated with a mint leaf is a perfect dessert. I also freeze some bags of blackberries for a pie or crumble in midwinter. A good blackberry liqueur can easily be made with half a bottle of vodka. Fill with berries to the top, add two teaspoons (ten mL) of sugar. Shake well and store for a month or so in a dark cupboard. Strain with a fine strainer and rebottle in a clean sterilized bottle. Serve in tiny glasses and savor the juicy taste of summer in December.

We do leave the garden occasionally during the season. We take our rowboat, the two dogs, a bag of chopped herbs, a bottle of wine, and a pizza from Sorrento's, the little Italian café in Brentwood Bay. We are good sailors and stand in the bow and watch other boats and gaze longingly at any remaining pizza crusts. Senanus Island floats into view and I think, "What a perfect *Swallows and Amazons* island. We could land and make a little fire and cook eggs in the frying pan with butter and have bread and marmalade just like Susan, John, Roger, and Titty."

So the pleasures of summer unroll; sun, water, fresh fruit and vegetables, hammocks, guests, meals outdoors, boats, and the flourishing garden. A good summer is healing and restorative. It gives one bravery and energy to return to fall and winter work and life which is often more tedious and much less sensuous. This summer I vow to spend more time in the hammock reading and dreaming. I think of Gulf Island forebears who seem in every album and story to be sitting on beaches and having picnics and going out to sea in a rowboat to catch fish for dinner. I know their life was physically arduous but sometimes I dream of living their life at the turn of the century. No telephones, electricity, TV, indoor plumbing—but, oh, they did know when to stop working and make life a picnic.

One of my favorite summer cookbooks is *More Recipes from a Kitchen Garden* by Renee Shepherd and Fran Raboff. The following two recipes are adapted from this book.

Corn and Potato Salad

1 lb. (450 g) new potatoes
1 cup (250 mL) cooked corn (cut from the cob)
1/2 cup (125 mL) sour cream
2 tsp. (10 mL) caraway seeds
Salt and pepper

Steam or boil the potatoes until tender. Cut into 1-inch (2.5-cm) pieces. Add corn, sour cream, and caraway and gently toss together. Add salt and pepper to taste. Can be served hot or cold. Serves 4.

Creamy Grated Zucchini

2 Tbsp. (30 mL) butter
2 cloves of garlic, minced
6 medium zucchini, grated
1 Tbsp. (15 mL) chopped lemon thyme leaves
3 Tbsp. (45 mL) low fat sour cream
Salt and pepper

In a medium skillet, melt butter. Add garlic and sauté over low heat until fragrant. Add zucchini and lemon thyme and cook, stirring frequently until the zucchini is tender. Remove from heat, stir in sour cream, and season with salt and pepper. Serves 4.

The Butcher, the Baker, and the Fish Stick Maker

o food shopping said the editor who must be obeyed. I needed no encouragement to call upon a butcher, a baker, and a fishmonger to learn what I could about their individual arts. Those kinds of visits to me are reassuring and comforting. Perhaps it is the echoes of the Depression, which my parents were still talking about when I was a child, or the fact that Mother used to send me grocery shopping at an early age and just tall enough to see the top of the butcher's counter if I stood on tiptoe. Mr. Crisp was a dour man who would loom over the counter and regard me with a baleful eye as I gave him Mother's order. His shop had the traditional sawdust floor spotted with drops of blood, and carcasses loomed in the back cooler room.

I have no very early recollections of a baker because my mother baked her own bread up until the late forties. Big loaves of puffy white bread and round trays of sticky cinnamon buns made coming home from school a culinary event. Alas, progress came to the village in the form of a bakery. As soon as the baker opened his doors, mother put away her yeast and flour. She would much rather paint and garden and the new bread was delivered and very good. I still remember the small, dense loaves of brown bread lined up on the kitchen counter on delivery day. The best thing of all about the baker was his name—Mr. Garlick—although no garlic entered his baking in those days. The bakery took over an old church hall, and my father wryly said it was now making a greater contribution to village life as a bakery.

There was no fishmonger in our village. Fish was so plentiful you either caught it yourself or someone gave it to you. My mother was one of two women in the village who regularly fished for salmon. Together they would get up at 4 A.M. and venture out in a small rowboat to catch salmon and cod for their larders and have the pleasure of early morning hours on the water fishing and watching the sun come up with no one yelling "Mom!"

The Butcher

I began my research with a visit to Ronald Orr and Son, family butchers in Brentwood Bay. In 1979, the Orr family, Ronald and Caroline and their four children, emigrated from Glasgow to open their shop in Brentwood. Five generations of the family have been in the butchery business, and two of the children, Fraser and Rhonda, have now taken over the shop.

They buy only Canadian meat and nothing is prepackaged. Supermarkets buy block beef in bags, whereas the Orrs buy the whole carcass and Fraser bones it out. As I chatted with the Orrs I came to realize how much of the work is done by hand. They have many older customers who like small amounts and often come into the shop to buy one chop. Fraser and Rhonda know their names and their preferences. Many customers are from the British Isles and are very happy to see their national soul foods, for here you can buy haggis, Ayrshire bacon, blood pudding, homemade sausages made daily, Scotch eggs, Bridies, and steak and meat pies, all made by Rhonda, who was taught by her mother.

They buy only local lamb, which costs a bit more than New Zealand or Australian, but it's worth it. For a lamb barbecuing class

I bought local Orr's lamb, Australian lamb, and supermarket lamb and the Orr's lamb won all the prizes for flavor and tenderness. Fraser says he believes that the memory and the taste of quality are remembered long after the price is forgotten.

Their beef is hung for twenty-one days and any specialty cuts can be done for customers. One German lady brings in her German cookbooks and the Orrs do special European cuts for her. I once had the chutzpah to take in my own lamb leg from the freezer and ask them to bone it. Not an eyelash was batted and they boned my lamb beautifully. It is a special treat to have people go that extra mile for a customer.

The Orrs are, of course, great sources of information about meat. Rhonda suggests that beef is fine in the refrigerator for three days, but she feels pork and chicken should be cooked the same day as they are bought or else slipped into the freezer. Rhonda suggests using a thermometer when roasting beef because it takes the worry out of either having beef too well done or too rare. She roasts beef at 350°F (180°C) for twenty minutes per pound for well done, fifteen minutes per pound for medium rare, and ten minutes for rare. (Double the time per kilogram if you purchased a metric roast.) Then she adds another ten minutes to the cooking time and lets the roast sit for ten minutes before carving. She never salts the meat before roasting but will add garlic if friends like it.

To cook the Orrs' homemade sausages, Rhonda suggests starting them in a frying pan slowly so the skins won't burst, then raising the heat to make them crisp and brown on the outside— about twenty minutes in all. Some people boil sausages to remove fat, but Rhonda feels this also removes the flavor and besides, she says, her sausages aren't filled with fat so this isn't necessary.

When I asked what was the goofiest question Fraser had ever got from a customer, he told me that a woman had once asked, in all sincerity, what human flesh tasted like for she had heard it tasted like chicken. In his broad Glasgow accent, Fraser replied that he didn't know, but if the woman ever tasted it would she come back and tell him what it was like?

People drive out from Victoria to buy from Orr's. They come for the quality of meat and the personal contact. When I ask for a small fillet for dinner, it is cut by hand in front of me and carefully wrapped in brown paper. I get advice about cooking certain cuts and sometimes I prolong the chat just to hear the Scottish voices. I hope the sixth generation of the Orr family continues the family tradition for it is well worth preserving.

The Baker

Bread is very close to my heart, the staple food I could never give up. I read and study about bread and bake it quite often, and I also hunt for bread and will drive miles at the merest whispered rumor of a new bakery.

The Italian Bakery is certainly not a new bakery in Victoria; it is more of an institution. Two brothers-in-law, Virgilio Mosi and Michael Pozzolo, both married to the daughters of a baker in Torino, emigrated with their wives and children to Victoria; from Italy in 1978. Michael, who has a degree in pharmacy, missed the bread of his country so much that with his baker brother-in-law he opened the Italian Bakery. They have been a success since they opened their doors.

I spoke to Michael's son Alberto, who was home for two weeks from his accounting job in Toronto to supervise the bakery while his father went to Italy for a holiday. Alberto says they do everything as if it were for themselves. "If it is good enough for us, we will make consistently good bread and pastries." This philosophy is evident in everything, from the pastries wrapped in pretty paper and tied with red ribbon, to the prompt and friendly service.

Goods from the Italian Bakery mark the seasons and holidays of our lives. At Christmas, large panettones are baked, and the buttery fruit-filled bread stays fresh for weeks and is our favorite breakfast during the Christmas holidays. At Easter, the dove-shaped bread, the colomba, is eaten for Sunday brunch, and I buy chocolate eggs and lambs with surprise gifts inside. The profiteroles have become the standard family birthday cake and we put a large candle in the center of the balls of chocolate and cream.

But it is the bread that I think is the most important product of this family business. It is a true taste of Europe on the West Coast. The baguettes are dense and chewy and very substantial, and I love them for a dinner party or for soup and salad at lunch. Our daily bread is the whole wheat or the multi-grain, which I buy five or six loaves at a time and freeze because I have to drive fifteen minutes to the bakery (worth every minute). They use hard Canadian wheat flour, which is probably the best flour in the world. As part of their adaptation to their new country, they make sourdough in large rounds and twisted shapes.

Alberto started going to the bakery at the age of ten and loved being with his father. After high school, he almost stayed in the bakery but listened to his mother and went away to be educated. The children have all worked in the bakery and come and go, but Alberto has come back to work here, and added a cappuccino bar like his grandfather had in Torino.

Again, the theme of work done by hand was evident here. The

dough is mixed in big mixers, but each loaf is kneaded by hand. Bread is a variable and living beast and it changes with the weather, the humidity of the flour and, some think, with the temperament of the baker. This is called the "sweat of the palm theory," which means a handmade loaf can't be reproduced with automation because it lacks the human touch. This makes the bread more expensive than supermarket bread, but it depends on your priorities. Europeans spend much more on food than North Americans, but I think there is a growing sector of people who regard good bread as an essential part of daily life not just fuel for existence.

I love peering into the back of the bakery and watching the men and women working—their clothes and hair dusted with flour, their arms and hands moving, shaping, and making the daily bread. Bread is baked three times a day so you are assured of a fresh warm loaf. There is a generational, cultural pride in the bread here, which is such an addition to Canadian food.

Alberto's tips for storing bread are to ideally eat it in a couple of days and keep it in a plastic bag either in or out of the refrigerator. But for the best experience, eat it shortly after you get home, while it is warm. Remember, when all else fails you in life, there is still good bread.

The Fishmonger

With the strains of "Sweet Molly Malone the Fishmonger" in my head, I made the short drive to Sidney. At the end of a short pier, at the very foot of Beacon Avenue, in an old warehouse, one finds the Satellite Fish Co. Satellite was started here in 1964 by Don Norbury, a local boy who knew nothing about fishing. But he learned quickly, and this has been a very successful venture. Don feels the reason is he buys directly from the local fishermen and handpicks his product.

I love visiting the store. On the exterior of the building, during the summer, are large paintings by local artists. Seagulls wheel and scream overhead. When you walk into the big tin-roofed shed, you can see Don's two assistants, Ken Norbury (Don's nephew) and Kim Hayward, slicing and filleting fresh fish as it comes in off the boat. These two men must be two of the most skilled filleters on the island. Don told me of fish processors that now fillet by machine and how the fish is bashed and bruised. A skilled hand filleter, however, does not damage his product. Like butchering and bread-making, the traditional arts must be done by hand if the best quality is to be obtained.

Heaps of live crabs come in and I have found that if I take live crabs home and boil them with a bunch of tarragon in the water, the crabmeat is wonderfully sweet and succulent. Having the nerve to do the dirty deed took me years of courage-building, but if you are a coward, Satellite boils crab every day for you. Live prawns, fat and succulent from local waters, have been available all summer, and I take these little wigglers home and cook them for just one minute and shell them.

When I asked Don Norbury his tips for cooking fish, he said he loves his prawns cooked with chopped garlic and butter, his oysters smoked, and his salmon fillets seasoned with some seafood seasoning and quickly sautéed in butter, the flesh side first and then turned to the skin side. He puts a lid on for the last few minutes so the fish steams and stays moist. Spring salmon is his favorite, and he prefers cod for fish and chips as he says it is moister than halibut. I asked how long you should freeze fish and he said it depended on how fresh the fish was when it was frozen. He would only freeze fillets a month. A whole fish that has been glazed will last a couple of months. It depends on how much surface is exposed to the air.

Fish being the political issue it is today led us to talk about the future. Getting a good product and consistent supply isn't as easy as in the past. The fish are sometimes not there, and farm salmon is getting better, but the flesh is softer and will never take the place of real wild salmon. By July 1, he has customers longing for wild salmon. He hopes the Department of Fisheries will get a handle on the supply and demand so we do not end up with a defunct fishery, which would be a tragedy for the west coast of Canada.

Don says that if fresh, fish should last four or five days, especially if it is lying on ice and not wrapped up, for it should be allowed to breathe. So put your fish in a plastic bag, open at one end, on ice, and the moisture will stay in the fish. The strangest question Don has ever been asked was by a fisheries officer, who gazed at a pile of flaming pink crabs (which always turn pink when they are cooked) and asked when the crabs were going to be cooked.

I love visiting this simple old tin warehouse. Kim and Ken keep it spotless and are always hosing it down. The fish is always on ice in the glass case or on a big steel counter. The fillets are always cut properly with no bits and pieces hanging and no ragged edges; sharp knives are mandatory in this business. Kim and Ken cheerfully wrap your purchases in newspaper and give you cooking tips. On the counter is a tin, a fund for the staff's round the world trip. There are always coins in it.

I hope that we care for our fish stocks so places like Satellite Fish Co. can continue to exist and show us what a good product from the sea should be. I like buying close to the source and it makes me happy to see the fish boats tied up to the dock unloading because I like my crabs and prawns frisky and wiggling.

So, in the midst of massive factory food production, which seems so prevalent these days, it is reassuring to know that there are little pockets of obsessed individuals with high standards who continue to produce wonderful food for us. Search them out and you will improve the quality of your life. They certainly have improved mine.

In honor of my Scottish butcher, I am giving you the Scottish Leg of Lamb recipe adapted from Madame Benoit's *Lamb Cookbook,* which has been a constant companion to my lamb cooking for the past fifteen years.

Scottish Leg of Lamb

1 leg of lamb, 4 to 5 lbs. (2 to 2.5 kg)
1 Tbsp. (15 mL) salt
1 tsp. (5 mL) black pepper
1 tsp. (5 mL) dried rosemary or 3 Tbsp. (45 mL) fresh chopped rosemary
1/2 tsp. (2 mL) allspice
1 tsp. (5 mL) sugar
1/4 cup (60 mL) hot bacon fat

Rub the lamb with a mixture of the salt, pepper, rosemary, allspice, and sugar, and place in a pan. Cover with wax paper and let stand 1 hour at room temperature.

Pour the hot bacon fat on top and place uncovered in a 375°F (190°C) oven 25-30 minutes per pound (50-60 minutes per kilogram). When done, place on a hot serving dish and let stand 20 minutes in a warm place before carving. Make gravy clear or creamy as you prefer. Serves 6-8.

San Francisco Bread Pudding

There are many ways to use good bread that has gone stale. Grind it up in a food processor, freeze it, and you have instant homemade breadcrumbs with no preservatives. Or make croutons. Sauté cubed bread with a little olive oil and minced clove of garlic and add to your dinner salad. However, a wonderful way to use up stale bread is a traditional bread pudding. Nursery food is suddenly becoming quite trendy. This recipe is adapted from *San Francisco Encore,* an excellent cookbook by the Junior League of San Francisco.

5 oz. (150 g) stale French bread broken into small pieces

1 cup (250 mL) milk

1 cup (250 mL) heavy cream

1 cup (250 mL) sugar

4 Tbsp. (60 mL) unsalted butter, melted

1 whole egg

1 egg yolk

1/2 cup (125 mL) raisins

1/2 cup (125 mL) shredded coconut

1/2 cup (125 mL) pecans

1 Tbsp. (15 mL) vanilla

1/2 tsp. (2 mL) cinnamon

1/4 tsp. (1 mL) nutmeg

Lemon Rum Sauce (recipe follows)

Preheat oven to 375°F (190°C). In a large bowl, combine all ingredients. Blend well. Pour into buttered 11-by-7-inch (28-by-17-centimeter) baking dish. Bake for 45 minutes or until set. Serve warm with Lemon Rum Sauce. Serves 4-6.

Lemon Rum Sauce

6 Tbsp. (90 mL) unsalted butter
3 Tbsp. (45 mL) sugar
1/4 cup (60 mL) lemon juice
Grated rind of one large lemon
2 egg yolks beaten
3-6 Tbsp. (45-90 mL) rum

In a saucepan, combine the butter and sugar. Cook over low heat until well blended. Stir in the lemon juice and rind. Pour some of the butter mixture into the egg yolks and whisk to blend. Pour this mixture back into the saucepan. Whisk over low heat until slightly thickened. Stir in rum to taste. Serves 6-8.

Savary Island Barbecued Salmon

This barbecue recipe originally came from Campbell River and came with me to the cottage on Savary Island. First you catch a salmon or purchase one. Then with a sharp knife, cut salmon longways and remove the backbone and all little bones so you have 2 fillets with skin on one side. Marinate for several hours with half a cup (125 mL) of dry vermouth and a cup (250 mL) of soy sauce to which you have added 3 minced cloves of garlic. Marinate in a flat dish skin side up. Barbecue over hot coals 5 minutes, skin side down, longer if the fillet is thick. Throw some alder leaves on the coals while cooking for added fragrance. The skin will char and blacken and act like a cooking dish for the fish. Serve with little new potatoes and lemon slices. Delicious cold.

Strawberry Fields

he thought of eating strawberries always brings me mixed pleasure because I first feel pangs of guilt, and then shivers of delight. Like most guilts, this one goes back to my childhood. Every June I would venture out to the strawberry patch and, when no one was looking (difficult in a large family as someone was always looking), I would steal some of the ripest, juiciest berries. The main difficulty with this theft was I could rarely get away with it. My body inevitably betrayed me with the telltale lumps and the flush of hives. "Noël has been in the strawberries," my mother would comment, then get out the iodine bottle, the cure for hives then. My red splotches would turn yellow with the iodine, and if I was properly contrite, my name would be painted on my tummy with the sharp-smelling tincture.

Many writers and eaters of strawberries have got quite carried away in paroxysms of delight over the famed red berry. Read this quote from that staple lady of American cookery and the author of *The Joy of Cooking*, Irma S. Rombauer: "No one . . . has really experienced paradise on earth until he has plucked and eaten a clutch of tiny ripe wild strawberries, warmed by mountain sunshine."

This brings us to the historical fact that strawberries were growing in the new world and enjoyed by aboriginal people long before the first colonizers came. Virginia Scully, in her book *A*

Treasury of American Indian Herbs, discusses how North American Indians went on veritable strawberry sprees and seasoned their meats and made soups and teas with the berries. There was also a small wild berry in Europe that made its way through France to England. The fruit was small, though the flavor and scent were excellent. In the 1600s, the large boisterous American strawberry called the *Fragaria virginiana* was crossed with the smaller European berry and the hybrids that descended from this breeding are the ancestors of our present berries. Some berries from Chile arrived in the late seventeenth century and were also intermixed. By the nineteenth century in England, there were more than 600 types of strawberries, and commercial production was happening all over England, Europe, and North America.

Where I live on the Saanich Peninsula, one can find the remains of a once-flourishing strawberry industry. Berries were shipped off by the ton to Empress Jams on the Mainland, and there was a fruit winery that made strawberry wine and loganberry brandy that dissolved your fillings. Sometimes our small strawberry patch does not produce enough berries for us, and I wander up and down country roads in June looking for more. You have to get up early, for often by ten o'clock the ripe berries are gone and smug berry pickers are driving back to town dreaming of jam and shortcake recipes. You can recognize them because their lips and fingers are stained red.

My favorite farm belongs to Daphne and Brian Hughes on Chalet Road. Dedicated organic farmers, they produce the sweetest and best berries I have tasted. Daphne informs me that her favorite type is 'Rainier', which she feels has a special flavor and is red all the way through. She snorts at the California berries that arrive here for the winter; they have been sprayed many times, are often white and green in the middle, and have very little flavor. Daphne believes one-stop convenience shopping has killed taste and consequently people don't even know what a good berry tastes like.

Good, sweet, organic berries do not keep and should be eaten or preserved the day they are picked. Organic berries cost more because more personal effort goes into the growing. Weeds are pulled by hand and not sprayed with chemicals, and the digging and soil rejuvenation are also done by hand. But the search, the drive down the country road, the chat with the dedicated organic grower, the picking, and then the eating make it a wonderful pursuit of good food, and well worth the extra money.

Years of experimenting with jam recipes have narrowed my choice down to two. Our house favorite is from *The Joy of Cooking* and is called Red Red Strawberry Jam. This is a whole berry jam with a thickish syrup, and besides being divine on toast goes well with pancakes, waffles, and ice cream. Some years the syrup is thicker than others and I think it depends on the ripeness of the berries and the pectin they contain. Our other favorite is actually the freezer jam recipe on the Certo bottle because it has such a fresh flavor, especially if you make it the day the berries are picked. I like the speediness of freezer jam. The two recipes make a good contrast with their cooked and uncooked flavors.

There are hundreds of strawberry recipes in which you can smother these red treasures with cream, custard, liqueurs, cake batter, pastry, and ice cream. For me, the simplest is often the best: A bowl of just-picked berries, a bowl of fine berry sugar, and then sour cream, which is a tart contrast to the sugar and berry-sweetness. Serve a glass of dessert wine (Hainle is a good choice) and bliss out!

Besides all this sensuous pleasure, the strawberry has nutritional attributes. It is full of vitamin C and iron and low in calories. Medieval physic gardens grew strawberries for diarrhea cures, and wealthy ladies often bathed in crushed berries, using them to whiten their skin and ease sunburn. My favorite strawberry story is in a book called *A Calendar of Gardener's Lore: Revealing the Secret of the Walled Kitchen Garden* by Susan Campbell: "After a delightful afternoon drinking iced claret cup and eating enormous strawberries at Clifford Priory, the Rev. Francis Kilvert and his friends had great fun on the lawn, six cross games of croquet and balls flying in all directions. More claret cup and more strawberries were followed by the strange and solemn sight of a total eclipse of the moon. . . . We wandered up into the twilit garden and there among the strawberries, fastened to a little kennel by a collar and a light chain to keep the birds away was a dear, delightful white pussy. There were more cats chained to kennels near the back door."—July 12, 1870.

The origin of the word strawberry is believed to be strewberry because of the tendency of mother plants to strew baby plants about on runners. Over the years, the strew changed to straw. Izaak Walton in *The Compleat Angler* wrote the definitive comment on strawberries: "Doubtless God could have made a better berry, but doubtless God never did."

Strawberries and Grand Marnier

This is an excellent way to enhance berries that are not quite perfectly sweet.

4 cups (1 L) sliced strawberries
1/4 to 1/3 cup (60 to 75 mL) sugar, according to taste
1 Tbsp. (15 mL) grated orange rind
1/4 cup (60 mL) Grand Marnier

Combine all ingredients and chill at least 1 hour before serving. Makes 6 servings.

No-Cook Strawberry Freezer Jam

4 cups (1 L) ripe strawberries
4 cups (1 L) granulated sugar
1 box powdered pectin
3/4 cup (175 mL) water

Wash and hull the strawberries and crush them completely, a few at a time. You should end up with 2 cups (500 mL) of crushed berries. In a large bowl, mix together the berries and sugar and let them stand for 10 minutes. Combine the pectin and water in a saucepan. Bring to a boil and boil 1 minute, stirring constantly.

Stir the hot pectin into the fruit in the bowl and continue stirring for 3 minutes. Don't worry if the sugar has not completely dissolved.

Ladle the jam into freezer containers. Put the lids on immediately. Let the jam stand at room temperature for 24 hours, or until set. Refrigerate to keep a few weeks or freeze to keep up to a year. Makes 2 1/4 pints (about 1 L).

Strawberry Cultivation

Strawberries grow well in the cool, moist conditions of coastal British Columbia and the Pacific Northwest. Choose a well-drained site with sun for more than half a day. The berries like a slightly acid soil rich in organic material. Purchase the young plants from a nursery so that you get virus- and pest-free stock. I once made the mistake of accepting some free plants from a commercial grower and got some free pests as well. Late spring is a good time for planting, but potted-up strawberries can be planted throughout the summer. Plants fruit better the second year if the first year's flowers are removed. When planting young rootstock, the roots should be distributed on the sides of a ridge of earth and then covered with an inch or two of soil well pressed down.

When the soil starts to dry out, I put straw on the soil of the bed. This keeps the topsoil moist, keeps the berries off the earth, and provides organic material for the soil. If the topsoil was well manured or composted at planting, the bed should be good for 2 or maybe 3 years of good eating. Some gardeners keep beds going for a longer time by allowing the runners of the old plants to root and then removing the old plants after their second or third fruiting.

—Andrew Yeoman

Supplying Herbs to Restaurants

id-life crises can take one down many paths. My husband and I took the garden path, surrounded by sweet smelling herbs.

Fifteen years ago I was ensconced in a junior high school library and Andrew was behind a desk giving advice about oil and gas investments when we jettisoned our careers and bought ten acres on the Saanich Peninsula and began to plant herbs.

We did no market research, but reading, traveling, and eating suggested that herbs—especially fresh ones—were going to become important in the restaurant business. The first two summers Andrew re-organized, terraced, and planted the garden, and we collected tarragon, sage, sorrel, several varieties of mint, oregano, and rosemary. I imagined myself in a flowing cotton dress, with a straw hat and wicker basket, daintily knocking on a restaurant door and offering my wares. In reality, I dressed in jeans, arrived in a pickup truck, and stood next to the garbage cans in a dirty alley, carting armloads of flats to call at the back doors.

In the spring of 1981, we sent four letters to restaurants we thought might be interested in fresh herb delivery. One chef answered and with great excitement we planned our first delivery. Then Andrew was struck with appendicitis and had to be hospitalized. Somehow I managed to put together our first order. The young chef was pleased and I was proud as he admired the herbs spread out on his kitchen counter. We did not have this customer long; his boss decided the gardener could plant herbs outside the kitchen door.

Weeks passed, the telephone began to ring, and our clients increased in number. A French chef came to visit and was thrilled to see shallots coming up and a bed of lush tarragon waving in the breeze. His father had been a market gardener in France and he was filled with nostalgia.

Gradually, we learned which plants grew well on our south-sloping site, how much we could cut the plants and how often to fertilize in order to cut again in a few weeks. Because we decided to go the organic route, our garden often reeked of fish fertilizer and blood meal. Consequently, so did our two dogs. Watering was done by hand with a wand, which gave Andrew a closer connection to the plants and enabled him to observe them carefully. Basil, for example, was new to us and we soon learned that cool nights on the coast are not what tropical basil likes. After trial and error, Andrew strung plastic tent tunnels over plastic irrigation pipe and the plants began to thrive.

My penchant for animals helped increase our supply of organic fertilizer. Soon we had twenty brown hens and five woolly sheep from Salt Spring Island.

As the years went by we became attuned to the chefs' needs and grew accordingly. The second year we pulled up a bed of tarragon. The French chefs would buy lots in September and would put it in crocks of white vinegar for winter, but that was all. We sold little sorrel the first few years but later it was in great demand for fish recipes and soups. Basil became the most important crop; ours is grown outdoors in rich organic soil and has a wonderful flavor. We sell it by the basketful and its exotic perfume permeates my hands, the house, and the truck—as well as a restaurant customer's dinner.

Chives are the most labor-intensive work as each yellow speck has to be removed before they are bundled and weighed. This takes several hours and the house and I smell of the gentle oniony herb. We also collect and package chive flowers to decorate plates or perk up salads. On a hot sunny afternoon, picking the fragrant herbs is a sensual and perfumed experience, but rainy days are difficult as wet chives quickly become slimy and moldy once picked. If it rains, we rush out and pick, then lay the chives out on thick beach towels on the kitchen counter and blow them dry with the hair dryer.

Friday is "herb day." We get up early, clear the dining room table, cover it with newspaper, and place our scales upon it. We phone chefs the day before and have a picking list ready to go. Andrew—the precise member of our partnership—does all the weighing, measuring, and accounting. He sits in our dining room, which has French doors opening out to the garden, and calls out if he needs more pickings. By 3:30 or 4:00 P.M. our herbs are bagged in plastic and paper and we hit the shower to get ready for deliveries.

Contact with chefs is one of the most satisfying parts of the herb trade. Our favorites are chef-owners because they pursue quality food purchasing and get excited about beautifully grown, pungent herbs. They stick their noses in the bags, take long sniffs of pleasure, and munch sprigs with relish. This is what gives a grower real pleasure and makes the labor worthwhile—just to see the contented smile on a chef's face.

I'm a rather snoopy person, especially when it comes to food and kitchens, and I find it fascinating being in restaurant kitchens late in the afternoon. I often taste delicious things, or observe food being prepared with impressive speed and skill.

As our business increased, I asked a chef how he found out about us. He laughed and said chefs meet after work, drink wine, gossip, and swap names of suppliers. When we were serving twenty-six restaurants, we reminded ourselves that small is beautiful and we cut down our number of customers to twelve. Then we started opening on Sunday afternoons so people could come to our garden and buy small plants. I wrote two herb cookbooks and began to give cooking classes. Andrew thinks I began to write to get out of weeding. He became involved in campaigns to save farmland and helped organize a local farmers' market.

The herb revolution is in full swing now, and many younger people are getting involved. We started years ago with a book called *Profitable Herb Growing at Home* by Betty Jacobs who once ran Jacob's Ladder, the first herb farm on Vancouver Island. I recommend her book if you are thinking about starting a herb business. They need little space—a city lot can grow sufficient herbs to supply several restaurants.

When delivery days are over, we usually go out to dinner and squander some of our profits. And if we dine at one of our customers' establishments, I often recognize, resting on my plate, a sprig of lemon thyme I picked earlier that afternoon. This gives me pleasure and again convinces me that it was indeed a good decision to tread down that garden path.

Baked Halibut with Sour Cream and Chives

We all know about sour cream and chives on halved potatoes. Try it with
halibut and serve a baked potato on the side.

4 halibut steaks, approximately 1 inch (2.5 cm) thick
Freshly ground black pepper
2 Tbsp. (30 mL) butter
2 cups (500 mL) sliced mushrooms
1 cup (250 mL) sour cream
1/4 cup (60 mL) dry sherry
4 Tbsp. (60 mL) chopped chives

Preheat oven to 400°F (200°C). Put halibut in a buttered 8-by-12-inch
(20-by-30-cm) baking dish. Season with pepper. Melt butter in a skillet
and sauté mushrooms for 3 minutes. Add sour cream, sherry, and chives
to skillet and mix together. Simmer for 1 minute, then pour mixture
over halibut. Bake in preheated oven for 25-30 minutes or until fish
flakes. Serves 4.

Sorrel Salad Dressing

Delicious on tomatoes, tuna salad, or chicken.

1/2 cup (125 mL) washed sorrel leaves
1/4 cup (60 mL) half-and-half cream
2 Tbsp. (30 mL) cream cheese
1 Tbsp. (15 mL) freshly squeezed lemon juice

Put all the ingredients in a blender or food processor and purée. Transfer to
a bowl and chill in refrigerator until ready to serve. Garnish with finely
chopped sorrel leaves and serve separate from salad. Toss salad with
dressing at the table. Makes 3/4 cup (175 mL).

The Egg and I

xcept for my twenties and thirties, when I had an urban existence, I have always had chickens in my life. One of my first childhood pets was an independent-minded brown hen called Pat, who refused to lay her eggs in the provided-for nest in the henhouse. Instead, she made her nest in the ancient horsehair-stuffed couch stored in the back of the garage. I was rarely able to collect her eggs as the springer spaniel, Sam, scoffed them before I did my egg collecting in the late afternoon. He would have eaten them for an early morning snack.

When we purchased our farm fifteen years ago, ten brown hens were included in the purchase price and there was a proper henhouse in the barn with neat rows of nests. I quickly learned that besides feeding the hens pellets, scratch, and food scraps, they had to be locked up every night at dusk, or marauding raccoons marched in and had chicken for dinner.

One night I forgot and woke the next morning to a horrible massacre. Parts of murdered hens had been dragged all the way to the orchard. We replaced the lost hens with some "new brownies," and I had an orgy of egg cooking that summer. The brilliant yellow yolks and the dense whites, plus the fresh eggy flavor, made me realize what I had been missing for years buying my eggs at the store. I made little pots of crème caramel for every guest, and I made soufflés, stuffed eggs, poached eggs, fried, and scrambled. I put bowls of brown eggs in pottery bowls on the counter and gazed at the newfound still lifes decorating my kitchen.

I quickly fell into a routine, one of those natural rhythms of rural life; I would visit my hens twice a day, first to let them out into their meadow where they roamed with the sheep, then at dusk to gather the eggs and lock the brownies up for the night. Occasionally, an intrepid hen would refuse to come in and would roost in the woodpile leaning against the barn. The next morning I would do a head count to see if there had been a raccoon attack. The hens were supposedly not to leave the fenced meadow, but some of them became explorers and ventured into the garden. The sheep dog, who had a natural herding instinct, was quickly trained to herd the hens back into the field. Hens may not be particularly bright, but they're not stupid either. Soon they could be seen flying over the stone wall clucking hysterically whenever they caught sight of the dog lumbering towards them.

When there is an overabundance of eggs, I give them to friends. Often their citified children object to the stronger flavor of eggs brought up on a meadow diet. So used to pallid supermarket eggs, they find the intense Provençal yellow of the yolks too vivid an experience.

Yet some people will drive for miles to buy eggs. They arrive in the country with a gleam in their eye. These are the serious egg hunters—exploring country roads for the "fresh egg" signs, then hopping out of their cars and running to the stand to see if there are any left.

The brown egg/white egg controversy is rather like the small Endians and the big Endians battle in *Gulliver's Travels,* where people fought over which end of a soft-boiled egg should be topped. There is a rural myth promoted by those of English descent that brown eggs are more nourishing. White eggs laid by white hens are used commercially because the white hens are more prolific layers, but the truth is they have the same food value. I much prefer brown eggs because of a childhood bias, and the aesthetic appeal of brown eggs, which somehow look so earthy and beautiful sitting in a basket.

Hen fruit—the perfect food in the perfect container—has been a nourishing comfort to humans since the first egg was stolen from a bird's nest. Linked with myths of fertility and the eternal female, eggs have always attracted us, and not always for their food value. Visual artists and culinary artists have made eggs from all kinds of materials: chocolate, pastry, marble, papier mâché, wood, gemstones, and precious metals.

I love painted Ukrainian Easter eggs, which are symbols of rebirth during a traditional religious holiday. But eggs are also a tangible link to the natural world because they are so beautiful to touch and cradle in your hands. To place a new-laid warm egg against my cheek is an amazing experience and makes me happy to be alive. The smoothness and the feel of the perfect curve against one's skin has universal appeal.

But on to more practical matters. For me, eggs are the perfect quick supper. Often on returning from a trip—jet-lagged and confused—we cook boiled eggs (five minutes in boiling water at sea-level) served with brown toast and Earl Grey tea. This simple meal is most comforting and makes me feel connected to the farm and my hens again.

My daughter lived in a house in Australia where three hens were kept by the family in the back garden. Inside their small house was a Kentucky Fried Chicken poster meant to urge the hens (or chooks, as the Aussies call them) to greater laying feats. Hens have been included in novels by famous Canadian authors such as Margaret Atwood, who in her novel *The Robber Bride* includes a riveting scene in which the departing lover nastily cuts the throats of his girlfriend's much-loved hens.

After several years of luxuriating in an unlimited supply of fresh eggs, my doctor measured my cholesterol and said, "Tut-tut." Oat bran entered my life, and now I have one egg on Saturday morning. This is a culinary high point of my week, and I cook it with great reverence and savor each mouthful. It has become one of my life's reliable pleasures, that Saturday morning egg.

On my birthday I am served a very special dish: perfect, creamy scrambled eggs with finely chopped chervil topped with a dollop of caviar, served with brown toast fingers and accompanied by champagne with fresh-squeezed orange juice. This is utter eggy birthday bliss.

While eggs are certainly one of nature's small miracles, hens are often derided as being stupid, flighty, dirty, and dusty. They are all of those things, but they are also amusing, companionable, and producers of a nourishing and perfectly balanced food that is inexpensive and delicious. *Larousse* has eight pages on eggs, and tells of how eggs were forbidden during Lent, then collected on Easter for prodigious consumption over Eastertide. I'll close this eggy dissertation with lines from an appropriate nursery rhyme:

Gentlemen come from miles away
To see what my black hen doth lay.

Bloomin' Edibles

few years ago I began to explore the subject of edible flowers and was surprised to find a real little controversy brewing. Most women who are into food and decoration love them. They read the books, attend the lectures, grow the flowers, and eat them with great pleasure. Men, however, tend to find the whole subject slightly weird. They seem squeamish and even cringe when you suggest eating these delicate objects of beauty. Perhaps this harks back to childhood when their mothers yelled at them not to pick or eat the daisies. I think some men feel it is unmanly to eat such things.

I recall one evening at Sooke Harbour House (where edible flowers are cooked and treasured) with a Scottish friend called Alistair. Alistair was famous for his love of potatoes and that night he clearly did not think he had got enough. So his wife and I plonked our potatoes onto his plate to silence him. Still, the extra starch wasn't enough to quell the heady combination of wine and the flowers in his salad. Alistair suddenly reached for the vase of flowers on the table and began offering them to other guests. The moral of the story became very clear to me. Some men get nervous and silly when their plates are bedecked with blossoms, so be careful where you take them to dine.

Sinclair Philip, who probably knows more about the subject of edible flowers than anyone else I know, told me another story about men and flowers. This particular night the Countess Mountbatten of Burma had come to dine with three Canadian generals and their aides. The countess was very knowledgeable about food, flowers, and wine (she chose B.C. wine), and she instructed the generals in what to order. When the famous flower salad appeared, one general was heard to say to his aide, "What would the men in the barracks think if they saw us eating this?"

I have no answer to that question, but I can tell you that women *and* men have been eating flowers for centuries. Before the Crusades, flowers, herbs, and salt were the main flavoring ingredients for food. Exotic spices were unavailable, and cooks depended on flowers and herbs for taste and as vitamin and mineral supplements. The Japanese have always used flowers in their cooking, and country people in Europe have never stopped. Sinclair Philip told of the village where he lived in France and the incredibly close relationship the people had with the plants of the countryside and the plants from their gardens. Blossoms, berries, and leaves are harvested all through the year to go into the soup pot, the salad bowl, and into teas or cordials for various seasonal ailments such as colds and coughs.

Mainstream restaurant cooking and home cooking in North America lost touch with the bounty of flowers in this century until the arrival of nouvelle cuisine in the sixties. Alice Waters of Chez Panisse fame in Berkeley, influenced by her time in France and the bounty of California and its agriculture, began an edible flower revival.

In an interview with Rosalind Creasy (the edible flower landscaping queen), Waters said, "The flowers are a fascination. People really focus on them and are very curious. Some people refuse to eat them, but about half will taste readily. I love to serve them in such a way that they are tasty and accessible to people; a large flower by itself is a little intimidating. I like to incorporate Johnny-jump-ups or nasturtium petals in salads or serve them in ice cream or butter."

Early in my edible flower researches I had an hour-long telephone conversation with Sinclair Philip, which was a mixture of academic lecture, hilarious stories, and food gossip. I asked the question all neophyte flower eaters want to know: what do they taste like?

Tuberous begonias, he told me, are eaten in forty countries of the world and have a sharp lemony taste. The colors, especially if crimson, add brilliance to sauces for seafood or dessert. Tulip petals vary in flavor depending on the amount of sun they receive while they are growing. They have a mild pea flavor. When put into a sorbet the colors seep into the syrup, creating edible art. Pansies add delicate color to vinegars and have a wintergreen peppermint flavor.

The smoky, vegetal taste of day lilies is stronger if grown in lots of sunlight. Chrysanthemums and calendulas can flavor rice, soups, and stir-fries with a pungent, spicy kick. Herb flowers are all edible, as are the flowers of vegetables that have gone to seed. Right now in our garden there are vivid yellow zucchini flowers and purple sprouting broccoli blossoms that will add a peppery zip to salads, soups, and stir-frys.

My first stumbling food-and-flower experiment was years ago when I made a chocolate cake for my daughter's first birthday. Somehow the cake when iced by my unskilled hands looked large, brown, and lumpish. Spying some calendulas blooming outside the kitchen window, I rushed out and picked some. I decked the cake with the flaming orange flowers. A true *bella figura* as the Italians say. It was not the usual pastel pink perfection for a dainty girl's first birthday, but she crowed with delight and I was pleased with my originality.

Years passed and a Chinese friend came to stay and offered to make her signature dish—Lily Petal Chicken. As she is named Lily, it all seemed a perfect example of culinary congruency. Dried lily petals (day lilies) are available in Chinatown. Soak them and use them for soups, stuffings, or in stir-fries. Fresh day lilies are used at Sooke Harbour House and have a chestnutty flavor with a hint of honey sweetness.

My next floral eating experience was with nasturtiums, and it was love at first bite. The peppery taste of the leaves, flowers, and buds, plus the strong flashes of orange and red and the ease with which they grow (barring the dreaded aphid attacks), make them my very favorite edible flower. A silver baked salmon laid on a bed of vivid green sorrel leaves with bright nasturtiums marching down the spine is one of summer's most wonderful sights. The Latin meaning of nasturtiums is "nose twister," for if you stick your nose into the flower it will make your nose quiver. The flower is often compared to watercress—sweet but pungent, peppery, and high in vitamin C. They are delicious chopped into omelets, stuffed with cream cheese, floating on pale green cucumber soup, stuffed in a vinegar bottle, scattered on a salad, tucked into tea sandwiches— the list goes on.

Roses were beloved in Roman cooking. They put them in wine, sauces, stews, and desserts, and scattered them about during their dining orgies. If you are cooking with roses, do not use ones from the florist for they have probably been sprayed with deadlies.

Use only an organic source of flowers. This applies of course to all edible flowers, and Rosalind Creasy, in the excellent chapter in her book *Cooking from the Garden,* advises one never to eat flowers you are unsure about. Many flowers are toxic and you should have an authorized list.

Two other inspiring flower-eating books are *The Forgotten Art of Flower Cookery* by Leona Woodring Smith and an English book titled *Cooking with Flowers* by Jenny Leggatt. Leona Smith's book has recipes using borage, carnations, chive flowers, chrysanthemums, violets, lavender, clover, dandelions, and roses. One recipe that struck me as particularly innovative was the lavender martini.

Jenny Leggatt's book is a visual delight. She uses flowers for weddings and special summer parties and has divided her use of flowers by food categories and festive holiday dinners. Such exotica as petal pastas, flower drinks, flower mustards, butters, and jams fill this charming book. One photograph of fresh cheeses on a plate, each with flower petals pressed into its surface, is truly spectacular. Calendulas, pansies, nasturtiums, and the green leaves of mint and cilantro are also used. Such a simple way to make an ordinary cheese plate rise above the humdrum using flower power.

Other flowers that I use every summer are the vivid star-shaped blossoms of blue borage. They grow easily and are pretty on salads, desserts, or frozen into ice cubes for long summer drinks. The red flowers of scarlet runner beans taste beany and add a gay hit of red when scattered over barbecued or grilled chicken. English daisies are charming on a plate of cucumber sandwiches for a summer tea. Violets look deeply dramatic on a bright yellow custard or on a pale sorbet. Lavender I have put in cookies and ice cream.

I asked Sinclair if he would send me his list of edible flowers and he promptly did. The fax machine kept grinding out page after page and I counted more than 100 flowers on the list. A few of the more unusual and unexpected were apple blossoms, cherry blossoms, mustard, radish, and squash flowers, and yucca blossoms.

Leona Smith feels the computerized world has pressed upon us too closely, too routinely, and many of us are returning to the use of our eyes, nose, and palate to seek pleasure in the enjoyment in food. Rediscover the beauty of food, she urges, through the forgotten art of flower cookery.

Edible Flowers

borage	gardenia	lime blossom	rosemary
carnation	gladiolus	marigold	squash blossom
chive	hollyhock	nasturtium	tulip
chrysanthemum	honeysuckle	orange blossom	violet
clover	jasmine	pansy	woodruff
dandelion	lavender	primrose	yarrow
day lily	lemon	red clover	yucca
English cowslip	lilac	rose	

Toxic Flowers

A few common garden flowers that are toxic and definitely should not be eaten are:

azalea	foxglove	oleander	wisteria
crocus	jack-in-the-pulpit	poinsettia	
daffodil	lily-of-the-valley	rhododendron	

Lily Petal Chicken

4 Tbsp. (60 mL) butter
2 boned chicken breasts, thinly sliced
1 cup (250 mL) sliced mushrooms
2-3 cups (500-750 mL) day lilies, cut into 1-inch (2.5-cm) pieces
1/2 cup (125 mL) chopped onion
1/2 cup (125 mL) snow peas diagonally cut into 1-inch (2.5-cm) lengths
1 1/2 Tbsp. (22 mL) cornstarch
1/4 cup (60 mL) chicken broth
2 Tbsp. (30 mL) soy sauce
1/2 tsp. (2 mL) ginger
2 Tbsp. (30 mL) dry sherry
1 Tbsp. (15 mL) honey
Salt and pepper

In a large skillet, melt butter, add sliced chicken, and cook 3-4 minutes, stirring to prevent sticking. Add mushrooms, day lilies, onion, snow peas, cornstarch dissolved in chicken broth, soy sauce, ginger, sherry, honey, and salt and pepper to taste.

Stir the ingredients in the skillet for 3-4 minutes or just until ingredients are fork tender but not exhausted. Serve immediately. Good with rice. Serves 4.

Flower Petal Butters

You can impregnate butter with the flavors of flowers by putting a layer of flowers in a glass dish and covering it with about 4 oz. (115 g) of unsalted butter, sliced in 2 pieces. Press the butter onto the flowers, then press more flowers around the sides and over the top of the butter. Cover with plastic wrap or foil and leave for about a day before using. If you are short of time, you can chop up lots of fresh, scented petals, mix them with butter and use immediately.

Stir-fried Fresh Crab with Ginger and Yellow and Red Nasturtiums

1 to 2 Tbsp. (15 to 30 mL) sunflower oil
8 spring onions (scallions) sliced
2-inch (5-cm) piece of gingerroot, grated
3 garlic cloves, crushed
1 Tbsp. (15 mL) chopped chives
White and brown meat from 1 fresh crab
Few drops of light soy sauce
3 Tbsp. (45 mL) mixed yellow and red nasturtium flowers
Chinese noodles or rice, to serve
Fresh nasturtium flowers, to garnish

Heat the oil in a wok until smoking. Toss in the onions, stir, and add the grated ginger, garlic, and chives. Reduce the heat slightly and stir-fry for a few seconds. Put in the crab meat and stir-fry for no more than 1 minute, until hot. Add soy sauce and the nasturtium flowers.

Serve on a bed of Chinese noodles or rice, and decorate with a flower or two. Serves 4.

Lavender Martini

Make your martini using your favorite proportions. Place a small sprig of lavender into the drink as the garnish. The oil in the lavender is quickly but subtly released by the alcohol, furnishing a new and appetizing taste.

Bountiful Basil

uly is one of my favorite months at Ravenhill Herb Farm, for that is when we have the annual unveiling of the basil (when the plastic covers are taken off), and the first picking. After that my cooking switches into basil mode and basil is included at nearly every meal. I even have basil jelly on whole wheat toast for breakfast.

Back in March, the basil plants were planted in trays and placed over a heat vent in the house so they would germinate in three days. (Basil needs temperatures of over 70°F [20°C] to germinate, so if you want to plant from seed in a coastal garden you have to wait until July.) The plants are set out in early May in raised beds full of compost and rich soil. A plastic row cover with holes poked through for ventilation is put over the plants and is left on until July, since coastal nights are usually too cool for these delicious aromatic tropical plants. They would rather be in Mexico or Maui.

After the unveiling in the garden, we have a ceremonial picking for the season's first pesto. Andrew carefully picks the leaves with a Zen-like reverence, then pulls out some early garlic and proceeds to the kitchen to make the pesto. He uses a fruity green olive oil, pine nuts, and the best Parmesan cheese from our favorite Italian deli where a lovely Venetian woman serves us the real thing in big chunks.

Andrew grinds everything up except the cheese in the food processor. If we were purists, it would be done with a mortar and pestle. I cook up some pasta, add bread and a simple salad, and dinner is ready. We usually serve a gutsy Italian or Chilean wine, something relatively young, without hard tannins but with a flavor as bold and straightforward as the basil itself. Then we sit out on the patio and enjoy the scent of basil, garlic, and cheese in the summer twilight.

We grow many types of basil, so sometimes we will make the pesto from the citrus-scented lemon basil. It tastes wonderful on fish or steamed vegetables, or tossed with bread and toasted pine nuts as a stuffing for summer squash. Almost any kind of basil can be made into a pesto except for purple ruffle basil, which turns black and is very coarse. Better to chop it up and toss it with greens in salads, or use it in a garlic-red wine butter sauce for pasta. Cinnamon basil is another favorite. It has small leaves and a reddish stem and imparts a hint of cinnamon to cream sauces. It is good with chicken, duck, and other poultry.

As summer progresses the basil becomes more luxuriant and plentiful. During the heaviest picking period we will give them some liquid fish fertilizer every two weeks and make sure that they get a good watering every two to three days in dry weather. Now I start to use basil with a liberal hand. I make bouquets of basil for the guest room and the patio table. I make basil burgers by placing a large piece of lettuce leaf basil on a bun and popping the grilled burger on top. I make golden brown loaves of pesto bread, which are pale green and speckled inside. (*The Italian Baker,* by Carol Field, contains an excellent recipe for pesto bread.) I flip basil leaves into stir-fries at the very last moment, and they turn a brilliant green.

My August lunch for days in a row is sliced, sun-warmed tomatoes from the garden lightly sprinkled with balsamic vinegar, a little olive oil, and some basil leaves chopped on top, then finished with a grind of fresh pepper. I even use basil as a dessert; it makes a wonderful ice cream. And although many of my guests pull a face at the prospect, I like to watch their expressions change from reluctance to delight after the first spoonful.

Basil beer bread is quick, easy, and delicious. Although it looks and tastes impressive, it contains only four ingredients and can be made quickly before lunch. A favorite salad is a warm wilted spinach and basil salad I adapted from *The Silver Palate Good Times Cookbook* by Julee Rosso and Sheila Lukins. The dressing contains that traditional winning combination of olive oil, garlic, Parmesan, and pine nuts. Nothing could be finer than to sit down to dinner with this salad, a crusty loaf of bread, some wine, and good company. The perfume of the basil leaves rises from the bowl, making one understand why the French use it as a perfume and the Cubans use it as a love potion.

One summer evening I gave a cooking class that included a dinner to celebrate the harvesting of garlic and basil. After the meal we all walked down to the vegetable garden and admired the rows of basil plants. The moon came up and one young man, obviously crazed by the heady combination of the moonlight and the basil, cried, "I want to roll in the basil." His friend quietly led him away.

Classic Pesto Sauce

2 cups (500 mL) freshly washed and firmly packed basil leaves
2-4 garlic cloves, peeled and crushed
1/2 cup (125 mL) olive oil
3 Tbsp. (45 mL) pine nuts
1 cup (250 mL) freshly grated Parmesan cheese

Put basil and garlic in a blender or food processor. Pour in oil and process until smooth. Add pine nuts and process for a few seconds. Stir in the Parmesan cheese. If the sauce is too thick, add more oil or a few drops of water.

If you are not using the pesto right away, put it in a jar in the refrigerator with a skim of oil on top and cover with plastic wrap. Pesto will keep for several weeks in the refrigerator, and it freezes well. To use, thaw slowly at room temperature.

Warm Wilted Spinach and Basil Salad

6 cups (1.5 L) fresh spinach leaves
2 cups (500 mL) fresh basil leaves
1/2 cup (125 mL) olive oil
3 garlic cloves, finely chopped
1/2 cup (125 mL) pine nuts
3/4 cup (175 mL) freshly grated Parmesan cheese
Freshly ground pepper, to taste

Mix the spinach and basil leaves in a salad bowl. Heat the oil over medium heat. Add the garlic and pine nuts and sauté until golden. Toss the oil mixture over the salad. Sprinkle with the Parmesan cheese and grind some fresh pepper over the greens. Serves 4-6.

Basil Beer Bread

One could experiment with many different herbs in this recipe. I first made it in the winter with rosemary.

3 cups (750 mL) self-rising flour
3 Tbsp. (45 mL) granulated sugar
1/2 cup (125 mL) basil, chopped
12 oz. (355 mL) warm beer

Mix all the ingredients together in a mixing bowl. Pour into a greased, regular-size loaf pan. Place in an unheated oven and set temperature at 350°F (180°C). Bake 50 minutes. Cool on a rack, then remove from pan.

Basil Ice Cream

2 cups (500 mL) milk
1/2 vanilla bean
1 cup (250 mL) basil leaves
4 egg yolks
1 cup (250 mL) sugar

Bring milk, vanilla bean, and basil leaves to a boil in a medium saucepan. Remove from heat, cover, and let steep for 10-15 minutes.

In a large bowl, whisk the egg yolks and sugar until thick and creamy. Strain milk to remove basil leaves and vanilla bean. Pour milk into egg and sugar mixture. Whisk well, pour into saucepan and cook over low heat, stirring constantly with a wooden spoon for 5-7 minutes. Cool. Freeze in an ice-cream maker according to directions. Serve with chocolate sauce on top. Serves 4.

Bodacious Corn

hen Christopher Columbus landed in Cuba in 1492, he was not looking for corn. Rather he was hoping for silks and spices and other Oriental treasures. To my mind he found a culinary treasure beyond compare—a truly North American vegetable.

Thousands of years before Columbus had his first corn feed, the Aztecs and the Maya had domesticated corn from wild grains. American Indians in their many different languages spoke of corn as "our mother and our life" or "she who sustains us."

Corn saved the lives of the first English settlers in Virginia after their crop failures, and corn was grown from the tip of South America to southern Canada. The yellow kernels capture the energy of the sun and turn it into delicious, nutritious food, containing vitamins A, B, and C as well as potassium and fiber.

A summer without corn would be unthinkable. I spend June and July thinking about corn feasts in August and September, and with every walk to the garden I measure its growth.

Our early corn is planted in soil blocks or peat pots in the house in the middle of April, and then in May it is put in a large cold frame, to be picked in mid-July if the weather is good. Corn, especially the super sweet varieties, if planted too early when the soil is still too cold, will rot instead of germinate. Main-crop corn is sown outside in mid-May. We use Territorial Seeds, for they specialize in seeds for cool coastal summers. Their catalog is a great source of information for coastal gardeners. Corn needs soil rich in compost and nitrogen because it is a heavy feeder. This year, Seneca Hori was the type planted for early corn and Miracle for the middle and late crop. Corn scientists are always working on new hybrids, and each year there is a new type of corn to try. Two of the latest hybrids are called 'Sugar Buns' and 'Bodacious'. How did *Playboy* get into the corn patch?

For me, a perfect summer meal is a large, steaming platter of just-cooked corn, some French bread, a salad, and maybe, if one is still hungry, a little something cooked on the barbecue. Meat as a centerpiece for a meal seems to fade in importance during corn season.

As all cookbooks will tell you, the pot of water should be boiling as you RUN to the garden with your basket and knife. The table should be set, the salad made, and the wine poured. Corn is ready to be picked when the silk tassels are brown and dry and the kernels look full. Stick a fingernail into a kernel and a sweet white milk should spurt out. The reason you are rushing is that as soon as you pick the corn, the sugar starts to convert to starch and the corn starts to lose its sweetness.

So, RUN back to the kitchen, shuck the cobs immediately, and toss them into the pot of boiling water. Timing for cooking varies. I usually cook them for five minutes, but some books suggest five to ten minutes. The older the corn the longer the cooking. Serve immediately with salt, pepper, and butter. Some purists reject butter and enjoy the pure corn flavor unsullied.

Often I make herb butters, which add another flavor dimension. As corn is wonderfully messy, provide lots of paper napkins or even damp facecloths. It is not a food one can eat with much elegance, but those who refrain from eating corn because of this are missing a true North American culinary experience. As a small child I remember an English great-uncle refusing corn at a family dinner and exclaiming in a shocked tone that corn was something fit only for cattle. Unfortunately, the only corn he had been exposed to was the coarse variety used for animal feed, but it was my first lesson in adult prejudice.

Some cooks roast corn in its husk on the barbecue or in the oven. After trying various methods I still prefer a simple boil or steam. I have tried to freeze corn on the cob and have found it disappointingly soggy. But corn kernels scraped from the cob and frozen are excellent and can be used as a vegetable or added to chowders or corn bread recipes. You can find corn scraping tools in kitchen shops but a good knife works just as well.

In early September, when we have had corn every night for several weeks, I start to think of various ways to use these sweet golden nuggets. I make corn pancakes, sometimes adding chopped bacon to them and serving them for breakfast with maple syrup, or as a side dish at dinner. Once in a San Francisco restaurant, I had corn pancakes served with roast duck. It was an enticing corn combination of crisp and crunchy textures. Corn bread with scraped corn added is another favorite and goes well with chili, baked beans, or soup.

Margaret Visser's chapter on corn in her fascinating book *Much Depends on Dinner* tells of American Indians planting corn with much ceremony and ritual. They performed dances to encourage fertility, and the women would shake their long hair to encourage the corn to flourish. I think I might go down to the garden this evening and dance around the corn plants shaking my hair. The corn gods should be thanked for providing us with such a nourishing golden food.

Corn Pancakes

If you're serving these pancakes for breakfast, serve them with maple syrup. For dinner, use them as an accompaniment to chicken, duck, or any grilled meat. They also make a good vegetarian dish when served with herbed yogurt (stir some chopped chives and parsley into low-fat yogurt).

2 1/4 cups (560 mL) corn kernels (approx. 6 cobs)
2 cups (500 mL) white flour
2 Tbsp. (30 mL) sugar
2 tsp. (10 mL) baking powder
Freshly ground pepper
3 large eggs
3/4 cup (175 mL) milk
2 Tbsp. (30 mL) butter, melted
5 strips of crumbled bacon (optional)

Scrape corn from the cobs and set aside.

Sift the dry ingredients together. In a separate bowl mix the eggs, milk, and butter. Stir in the dry ingredients. Mix until just moistened. Add corn and bacon bits. Ladle 4- to 5-inch (10- to 12-centimeter) circles of the mixture onto a hot greased pan, cook for a couple of minutes and then flip the pancakes over. Makes 10-12 pancakes.

Herbed Corn Bread with Fresh Corn

Corn bread is best when still warm, right out of the pan, so make this recipe just before serving. The corn niblets add moisture and texture to the bread. Fresh sage is a good substitute for cilantro or chives.

1 cup (250 mL) cornmeal
1 cup (250 mL) white flour
2-3 tsp. (10-15 mL) sugar
4 tsp. (20 mL) baking powder
1 egg
1/4 cup (60 mL) melted butter
1 1/2 cup (375 mL) corn kernels
1/2 cup (125 mL) chopped cilantro or chives

Mix cornmeal, flour, sugar, and baking powder. In a separate bowl, whisk egg and butter well. Add corn and chopped herbs to cornmeal flour mixture. Whisk in the egg and melted butter until the mixture is smooth. Pour into an 8-inch-square (20-cm) greased cake pan and bake at 425°F (220°C) for 20-25 minutes.

When cooked, cut into squares and serve while still warm. Also good when served with Cilantro Shallot Butter.

Cilantro Shallot Butter

This is delicious served with corn on the cob. You can make it the day before and then serve it at room temperature.

3/4 cup (175 mL) unsalted butter, room temperature
1/2 cup (125 mL) finely chopped cilantro
1 shallot, finely minced
2 tsp. (10 mL) fresh lemon juice
Several grindings of fresh black pepper

Purée all ingredients in a food processor or mix together by hand. Transfer to a bowl. Wrap and refrigerate.

Picking Friends

uests and the summer come together at our farm. The tepee we got in Alberta is unrolled and the lodgepole-pine poles, which stand in the garden all year as a kind of sculpture, are covered with the canvas. This is the guest room for the under-twenty-fives, who quite like it as no one knows when they come home from the pub. The two guest rooms upstairs are tidied up and new books and magazines put in place. We have two guest rooms at Ravenhill. One is filled with Victoriana and paintings of the young queen as well as early relatives of ours. The other sleeps six at a pinch and is called the girls' dormitory. Both have wonderful views over the valley and the garden and are very restorative places, as guest rooms should be.

Over the past fifteen years, there has been quite an array of guests in those rooms, from all over Canada, Japan, England, and other places. One summer I put up visiting children's authors for a literary convention and had a wonderful chance to meet them and get my books autographed. Jean Little, the children's author from Ontario, came with her new guide dog Ritz. Her older dog had been retired, and she and Ritz were forming new bonds. It was fascinating to spend time with this intrepid writer and her dog.

Overnight guests come and go quickly and do not really get involved with life on the farm and the garden. Then there is the other species of guest, like four English nephews who have come for long visits and finished many projects such as making an English stile so I can walk through the field, climb the stile, and land right by the mailbox. They have also dug holes for swimming pools, made raised beds, mended roofs of collapsing teahouses, and other such manual, manly tasks.

Fridays during the summer months are herb days, during which the herbs are cut for the chefs and delivered. Many a guest has been press-ganged into clipping the yellow bits off the chives and making neat, perfect bundles—a tedious job for one week's order of chives will take several hours. I have noticed some guests avoid coming on Friday and prefer to arrive on Saturday morning. One friend, after being forced into chive labor, developed a severe allergy to the onion family and begged off, though I noticed she happily ate chives in her salad and sandwiches.

There is a theme emerging here: Life and work go on at the farm, and guests often have to fit into that schedule. One friend, who was a hoverer and was always asking what she could do to help, picked a whole blackberry crop in several sessions. "Oh, go pick some more berries," I would say and provide myself with a few quiet moments alone in the kitchen. Well, she was the best blackberry picker in B.C. and she filled every pot I had. I started to make blackberry jam, blackberry pies, and blackberry ices. Our lips and fingers were stained purple, and the freezer groaned with the fruit. Finally, the guest left and I sank back into a blackberry-induced stupor.

Picking blackberries is the essence of a British Columbia summer. All along our country road in August, cars are parked and one can see people up stepladders, bottoms facing the road, plastic ice cream buckets dangling from wrists as they reach up for the highest berries. There is something very comforting about foraging for food—an atavistic experience that takes us back to our ancient, hunting/gathering ancestors.

My daughter's boyfriend came from England and asked for a task. He was given the job of attacking thistles and broom that threaten to take over the pasture. The sheep will not eat either, and Vincent Van Goat, who was purchased to do just that because we all know that goats will eat anything, does not deign to even nibble at these colonizing plants. Once he learned about alfalfa, he became a gourmet and is very selective about his diet. I even buy large sacks of broken carrots for him from the neighboring farm.

So guests of all ages are given tasks—shelling peas, picking raspberries, hulling strawberries, collecting eggs, scrubbing the goose pond, painting fences, cutting long grass, weeding, haying, and the most despised job of them all—cleaning out the henhouse.

Over the years there have been guests who have won my best guest of the summer award. A drama teacher called Ron, who loved to cook, came while the yellow plum tree was in full fruit. My mind boggled over the size of the crop. What to do with it? Ron picked the fruit, then sat on the patio and peeled and pitted it. The chickens got all the skins (and if I had been alone they probably would have gotten all the fruit). Then Ron searched through my 300 cookbooks and decided to make plum sauce.

A few hours later, summer yellow jars of plum sauce were lined up on the counter. It lent a wonderful spicy note to my winter cooking and got rid of my yellow plum guilt, with which I am usually afflicted each summer. Chicken breasts in yellow plum sauce have become a favorite dish.

Another useful guest is a retired Irish engineer, also called

Ron, who arrives and immediately looks for a tool kit. Then he
wanders through the house and barn, jiggling door knobs, tapping
loose drawers, checking dripping pipes. By the end of the visit, our
house is in much better shape. Doors close properly and hinges are
oiled. When his ladyfriend comes, she bakes the kind of apple pies
that only a prairie farm woman can make so well.

Another favorite guest is a therapist who listens to my tales
and enjoys her weekends in the country. She has been coming for
fifteen years so the exchange must be working.

Feeding guests can be arduous, but we now have a simplified
system. Breakfast and lunch are laid out on the counter, and guests
help themselves. There are always fresh brown eggs from the hens,
lots of homemade jam and herb-flavored honey, plus high-fiber
cereal for the middle-aged. Lunch is a big mix of salad greens and
vegetables from the garden. Guests can eat when and what they
want. At dinnertime everyone usually gets together and I barbecue
and cook whatever is growing in the garden. We eat lots of
tomatoes, salads, corn on the cob, and new potatoes. Of course
herbs are liberally applied to everything, including bread and
desserts.

Guests are good for the soul. They make me tidy the house,
spruce myself up, and think about the menus. They heighten life
because their remarks and conversation never fail to make you look
at your house and possessions and garden with new eyes. They
enter your domain and stir things up, which helps us to be
stimulated and not fall into ruts of middle age and hoary habit.
Sometimes, after they have gone and the sheets are laundered, I
relax into sloth and read for hours and have eggs and toast for
supper. But after a few days, I am bored and want to hear about

someone else's life and have a political argument at dinner and hear what someone else is reading and thinking.

I have loosened my hold on the kitchen and now love my guests to cook. Once some friends arrived with four children. He was a chef and she an artist who photographed and sketched the garden and the animals. The children found a secret nest of eggs, and their father made amazing, fluffy pancakes with the eggs, and apples off the Granny Smith tree. He also came armed with an enormous salami and a giant loaf of rye bread, which we all snacked on during the weekend. Not only that, they all helped with the dishes and the children were charming and peaceful. The coup de grace was that the chef had a hilarious sense of humor and told wonderfully dirty jokes. What more could the host and hostess ask?

Guests often bring gifts, and I think I speak for many hosts when I say the best gifts are wine and food. By the time you are a certain age you usually have enough objects. Because we have sheep, for many years people brought me sheep ornaments until I had a whole flock of motley-looking baas. I put them all on a windowsill in the guest room and it seemed to stop the guests' urge to give me sheep. I must admit a new kitchen gadget pleases, for I can never have enough.

One summer my daughter invited a friend and her new fiancé. The guest rooms were filled so we decided to make the tepee a little more glamorous. We lined it with an oriental carpet and large cushions. We put in a tiny table with a vase of scented roses and books of love poetry. Candles completed the stage set. The only disturbing element, however, was that they came in the next morning covered with mosquito bites and slightly disgruntled.

My final advice is to keep your meals generous and simple.

Suggest to the guests that you would love help with the dishes. Do not put up with that feeble excuse: "I would love to help but I don't know where anything goes." Get up early if you need some time for yourself. Alexander Pope has very sage advice:

> *For I, who hold sage*
> *Homer's rule the best*
> *Welcome the coming,*
> *speed the going guest.*

Noël's Chicken Breasts with Plum Sauce

4 single chicken breasts, skinned
1 1/2 cups (375 mL) plum sauce
Freshly ground pepper
1/2 cup (125 mL) rum, vermouth, or white wine
1/2 cup (125 mL) chopped fresh cilantro

Preheat oven to 350°F (180°C).

Place skinned chicken breasts in a flat baking dish. Sprinkle with pepper. Spoon plum sauce over breasts. Pour rum or wine over chicken. Bake 45 minutes and baste frequently. After 20 minutes, turn breasts over. When cooked, place on a warm platter. Spoon sauce over the chicken and sprinkle with chopped cilantro. Serve with rice or noodles. Serves 4.

Here are two quick and delicious recipes for your guests this summer. They come from Edena Sheldon's *Canada Cooks: Barbecue*. My copy is so spotted with olive oil and marinade it is getting difficult to read.

Fresh Basil Aïoli

This fresh, basil-flecked, green aïoli is delicious slathered over a sizzling piece of succulent grilled fish or chicken, hot off the coals.

3 cloves garlic, peeled and quartered
1 tsp. (5 mL) salt
1/2 cup (125 mL) fresh basil leaves, packed
2 egg yolks, room temperature
3/4 cup (175 mL) olive oil
1/2 cup (125 mL) safflower oil
1 Tbsp. (15 mL) fresh lemon juice
1 Tbsp. (15 mL) fresh lemon rind (yellow part only)
Freshly ground black pepper

In a food processor, purée the garlic and salt into a fine paste, scraping down sides with a rubber scraper. Add the basil leaves and process to a fine purée. Add the egg yolks and continue to process until smooth and completely incorporated. With the motor running, add the olive oil in a very thin, slow, steady stream beginning with a few drops. Continue with the safflower oil. Finally, add the lemon juice and rind and beat until smooth. Season to taste with pepper.

Store finished aïoli in a glass jar, tightly covered, for up to 5 days. Whisk smooth before serving. Serve chilled or cool. Makes 1 1/2 cups (375 mL).

Gingered Honey Barbecued Flank Steak

Flank steak teams beautifully with marinades, grills evenly, and when sliced on the diagonal across the grain, makes for a handsome presentation.

1 2-lb. (900-g) flank steak
2/3 cup (150 mL) vegetable oil
1/3 cup (75 mL) soy sauce
2 Tbsp. (30 mL) orange juice
2 Tbsp. (30 mL) grated fresh ginger
2 large cloves of garlic, peeled and pressed
4 Tbsp. (60 mL) honey
4 Tbsp. (60 mL) sherry wine vinegar
2 green onions, trimmed and finely minced

Place flank steak in a rectangular glass baking dish just large enough to accommodate it. Whisk together the oil, soy sauce, orange juice, ginger, garlic, honey, vinegar, and green onions. Pour half over the steak, turn meat, and cover with remainder of marinade. Cover and refrigerate steak 2-4 hours, turning meat 2 or 3 times. Bring to room temperature 20 minutes before grilling.

Lightly oil grill. Place steak over hot coals, 4 inches (10 cm) from source of heat. Grill 5 minutes per side for medium rare (meat should just yield when pressed). Remove meat from grill and allow to stand on cutting board 5 minutes before slicing.

Slice steak across grain, on the diagonal, into thin strips. Season with salt and pepper. Serves 4.

Mulch Music

ately I have been fascinated by all things circular.

While thumbing through my organic gardening books and thinking of the organic vegetables I have eaten over the past fifteen years, circular metaphors kept rising to the top of my composting mind.

I collect bread and food scraps (not meat) and take them out to my hens, who devour them and then produce beautiful brown eggs while at the same time fertilizing the straw litter in their pen, which is taken to the compost heap, which goes onto the vegetable garden, which produces the vegetables we eat, of which I take the remaining scraps to the chickens. . . . Round and round like the birth and death cycle—from decay comes rebirth.

My husband and I fell into organic gardening by way of books. Andrew, the gardener, read all the classical organic books by Laurence Hills, M. M. Vilmorin, and the not quite organic one by Steve Solomon. During our travels, we even tried to track down some of the organic gurus in their own gardens. We caught a glimpse of Hills at his retirement home at Ryton Gardens, The National Centre for Organic Gardening in England near Coventry. There he was, bundled in a heavy black overcoat, walking slowly through the organic plots on a blustery fall day—the man whose inspirational but very pragmatic books had inspired thousands to join the organic camp. We found Steve Solomon's garden in Oregon, but no one was home.

When we travel, we are really on a kind of philosophical/
gustatory/horticultural journey, each of us taking different paths,
mine through the kitchen and Andrew's through the garden. But the
paths are always entwined and connected in a circular way. The end
result has been a bountiful supply of vegetables for me to cook and
write about and a garden that has been a source of physical and
intellectual nourishment.

As the long days of summer begin to shorten and move
toward autumn, they bring golden days for the cook and also for
the guests at our farm each year. We eat corn, baby squashes,
yellow zucchini, green beans, and, of course, tomatoes. I am acutely
aware of the end-of-summer flavors. The yellow tomatoes are so
sweet and, dressed with a little basil, almost make a complete meal.
I find myself preparing very simple meals that focus on one
vegetable. Three cobs of corn, a piece of bread, and a glass of wine
are perfect for an evening meal. The fruit from our garden is also at
its peak, perfect for a summer breakfast: huge, ripe, scented
blackberries; fragrantly fleshed peaches; and, to my delight, six fat,
purple-brown figs from a tree I planted five years ago.

The common denominator that nourishes all this produce is
Andrew's compost and a policy of no insecticides or chemical
fertilizers. Yes, we get bugs occasionally (aphids and flea beetles),
but Andrew's theory is to grow enough for us, the chefs we supply,
and the bugs. Garden writer Helen Chesnut recently wrote about
putting extra compost on plants that were suffering from disease
and how the plants' health improved. An English cookbook called
The Cook's Garden by Linda Brown has a comment on the subject:
"No one seriously interested in eating good food would spray their
garden out of choice or subject them to impoverished soil. Plants
raised organically can have greater nutritional value."

Brown goes on to explain how vegetables have a state of perfection that is very brief. Gluts occur and the seasons provide the stimulus for our menus. The seasons also affect the taste of herbs and vegetables, she says. In the spring, the flavors are clean and astringent. In summer, there is more sweetness because of the sun and the soil. Years ago, my first artichokes were bitter and sharp. But now, because they are growing in richer soil and have more sun, they are sweet and don't have a hint of bitterness.

It is interesting to note that all farming was organic until about eighty years ago when massive amounts of chemical fertilizer began being produced and monoculture began. *The Vegetable Garden,* written by Madame M. M. Vilmorin (of the famous French seed house) in the nineteenth century and now reprinted in English by Tenspeed Press in California, is an amazing source of organic techniques and information and lists herbs and vegetables that have long been forgotten. Madame felt that a certain degree of openness to sun and air and good rich soil governed the flavor of vegetables. She snorted at gardeners who grew for size.

While reading an article on goat-cheese making, I came upon the word "terroir," or "earth." French cheese makers and, of course, winemakers know that the soil affects the flavor of cheese and wine. What the goat or ewe is eating, or what soil the vines are grown in, has a direct relation to the flavor of the end result. As a child, my mother purchased raw milk from a small dairy, and in late winter she would taste the milk and say with a sniff: "Mr. Laban is feeding the cows turnips." When the spring came and the cows were onto fresh grass, she would tell us the milk was better and to taste the cream floating on top—sweet and thick.

There has been much in the press recently about genetic tampering with the tomato. Growers can now produce a tomato that has a very long shelf life and is still edible. There has been an outcry from such organic purists as Alice Waters in California, and many famous restaurant chefs vow they will never use these tomatoes in their cooking. Waters believes good cooking begins with good ingredients, ones that are fresh, ripe, seasonal, and unadulterated by spray or chemicals. She strongly asserts that such ingredients will give your cooking more integrity as well as a more lively taste. And because you are eating seasonally, life becomes more circular and congruent due to your connection with food and the earth it comes from. If you do not have a garden, you can still search out local markets and growers and ask your stores to carry local organic food.

Several years ago we dined at Chez Panisse in Berkeley—Alice Waters's famous restaurant. I still remember the pumpkin soup and the orange chanterelles. It was a crisp fall evening and the brilliant orange fall food of mushrooms and pumpkins fit the season to perfection. Waters has been a leading advocate of organic growing for restaurants and has formed organizations to help make the connection between farmers and chefs. This is beginning to happen on Canada's west coast as well and this makes me very happy.

There are metaphysical and spiritual overtones in the organic camp, which are quite understandable. After all, there is little satisfaction found in reaching for a package of frozen or much-traveled vegetables. Do you know where your vegetables come from and what has been done to them? Think about it.

Pumpkin Soup with Pancetta

2 lbs. (900 g) fresh cooked pumpkin
3 cups (750 mL) scalded milk
1 Tbsp. (15 mL) butter
2 Tbsp. (30 mL) brown sugar
Salt and pepper, to taste
Pinch of nutmeg
Pinch of cinnamon
2 to 3 threads of saffron
4 slices of pancetta ham

Combine the pumpkin with the milk. Add butter, sugar, and spices. Heat but do not boil.

Fry pancetta slices until crisp. Crumble on top of soup. Makes 4 cups (1 L).

Rural Compost Cake

2 parts: grass, hay (if unsprayed), green plant material, vegetable and fruit kitchen waste
1 part: dry leaves, sawdust (not more than 10 percent), straw, chopped or shredded woody stems, chicken, sheep, or cow manure
Additives: water

Spread the material in layers 3-6 inches (8-15 cm) thick, alternating between green (nitrogen rich) and brown (carbon rich) layers, to make a pile at least 3 cubic feet (1 cubic metre). The pile should be kept thoroughly moist as it is built, but don't keep it so moist that water leaks out of the bottom of the pile.

The pile should be covered with black plastic. If the mixture is right, it will heat up to about 150°F (70°C) within 2 days. It should be turned after 3 or 4 days and then turned again into a storage bin after another 4 or 5 days. It is ready to use in 3 weeks. If it does not heat up strongly, then the pile can be turned into storage and will be ready to use in 3 to 6 months.

Urban Compost Cake

2 parts: grass clippings (unsprayed), green plant material (chopped if stemmy), kitchen waste (no meat)
1 part: dry leaves, sawdust in small amounts, chopped or shredded woody stems
Additives: water, garden soil, blood and bone fertilizer. A general fertilizer can be used but it should be high in nitrogen and phosphorus.

Layer the mixture, sprinkling each one with several handfuls of soil and a handful of fertilizer. The mixture can be layered in a pile surrounded by strong wire mesh or within a rat-proof (metal or very heavy plastic) commercial container. Decomposition will speed up if the pile is mixed or turned. It should be ready to use in 2 to 4 months.

—Andrew Yeoman

Steve Solomon's Not-So-Secret Fertilizer Formula

This mixture comes from Steve Solomon's *Growing Vegetables West of the Cascades*.

4 parts seed meal or fish meal
1 part dolomite lime
1 part rock phosphate or 1/2 part bonemeal
1 part kelp

Lime is included in the mix to offset the acidity of many seed meals. Dolomite lime contains both calcium and magnesium, essential plant nutrients.

Mix the fertilizer in a big garden cart or on a tarp spread on the driveway. Simply dump out the stuff by the sack and blend it by turning it with a shovel until it's a uniform color. Then shovel it into a large garbage can with a tight lid or back into the empty sacks for storage and use as needed.

Mists and Mellow Fruitfulness

o write about October without thinking of the poet Keats is impossible for me. The oft-quoted lines of mists and mellow fruitfulness, moss'd cottages, trees bending with apples, ripeness to the core, bees buzzing, and swelling gourds all capture the feeling of autumn.

October at the farm is a quiet reflective time for we close the gates, the herb season is over, and the place returns to us and the animals. Henry, the ram, after a summer of being by himself in a field and pacing the fence that keeps him away from his ladies, is now allowed to be with them again and he is calm and peaceful, his restless pacing done and we hope next year's lamb crop secured and begun. The sheep are all in the field we call the old orchard and they patiently wait under the trees for the apples to drop. The grass is yellow and burnt after the long hot summer and there is an edge to their appetites.

Apples are abundant and because they are unsprayed they make wonderful juice for freezing. Sometimes if there is a large crop we take them to a neighboring farm, which has an enormous press, and let them make the juice. We cart it home in the truck with lazy wasps buzzing and banging against the sticky bottles. I make applesauce to freeze for roast pork dinners in the winter and maybe an applesauce cake for a rainy day tea.

The last local farmer's market in early October has the feel of a country fall fair about it. I load up on exotic-looking squashes, turbaned with orange stripes, or green, yellow, and pale spotted ones. I wash the squashes when I go home in a gallon of water with a tablespoon of bleach in it; this stops them from rotting so I can then stack them in bowls on the wooden kitchen table and enjoy the orbs of color and the comforting thought of future dinners. There is an air of nostalgia at the last market, and the camaraderie of the stall vendors has a note of sadness for they won't set up their tables again until next June. I buy pots of jam made from fruit I don't have and jars of pickles and relishes I cannot resist. A crispness defines the air and though the sun still shines, the heat of summer is now just a memory.

Thanksgiving arrives and there is such an abundance of fruits and vegetables that a turkey seems redundant. Perhaps I should cook squashes, potatoes and turnips and shape them into a turkey mold, glaze it golden brown and thank the fertility goddess for all the fruits of the earth. I make my annual pumpkin pie and always use the same recipe from *The Joy of Cooking* called Pumpkin Chiffon Pie. It is light and fluffy and rests on the stomach easily after a large turkey dinner. A niece of mine once mentioned that she loves Thanksgiving because there is no Christmas pressure and no frenzied gift-giving and I must say I sometimes agree with her.

But Christmas is a ways off yet and in October I have the atavistic urge to fill the larder. I make sun-dried tomatoes in my little convection oven. They dry overnight and are little daubs of intense future flavor in my winter cooking. On our walks with the dogs we hunt for mushrooms, and sometimes if we drive up the island we find a mushroom station and buy a bag. I bring them home and cook them in a little unsalted butter and freeze them in jars. A supper of orange chanterelles on brown toast is the perfect autumn meal with a baked apple for dessert.

Andrew stores the garlic, the shallots, and the potatoes in the cool garage and in the barn. This will last us until March, when the potatoes start to sprout in the dark and the garlic grows little green shoots; tiny hints of spring that encourage one after a long rainy winter.

October is a time of gleaning in the garden. There are always a few tomatoes on the withering vines, either green, yellow, or red. I love fried green tomatoes, which the Mennonites and the Italians cook. Gardening in Alberta for a few years made me appreciate the firmness and the acidic tang of green tomatoes. They are delicious fried with bacon and eggs, or dipped in cornmeal and baked, made into jam, pickles, relish, or pies laced with brown sugar, cinnamon, and cloves. I search the sorrel patch and garner some tart, green, lemony leaves to purée and freeze for a potato soup in the winter. Adding sorrel to a basic potato soup enlivens this dependable starch with a lemony zing.

Years ago we brought home some pumpkin seed from France and have been growing them ever since. Every year, Andrew saves more seed to ensure a fresh crop. This variety makes a lovely pumpkin soup, which is very comforting on a cool winter day, especially when topped with some garlicky homemade croutons. The pumpkins sit patiently around the kitchen until it is their time to be cooked, adding a hit of brilliant orange color to my decor.

October is housekeeping time in the garden. The lawn furniture is put away in the barn with some sadness for it is a signal that another season is over, and I have regrets that I did not sit on them more often last summer and stare at the view. Actually, the view over the valley has widened as the leaves fall off the copper beeches. Fall brings a different beauty with widened vistas and bare branches.

Leaves are raked and dumped into the leaf-mold bin where they will rot down in the winter rains and be put on the garden in the spring. The circular path of nature repeats itself again and again in the garden. Rot, nourishment, and rebirth. We mulch tender plants in the garden such as lemon verbena and the bay trees. This helps in case we get a deadly freeze. New rosemary plants can take a little mulch also until their roots get established. The mulch can be straw, leaves, or bark mulch. Cover up your tender exotic babies for the winter.

I snip a bag of lemon balm leaves and lemon verbena to dry for tea. This makes a wonderful tea after dinner—a digestive and a sleep inducer. I also make preserves for Christmas presents, a port wine jelly that is a favorite for ham and turkey, vinegars of various sorts, raspberry, blackberry, and tarragon, for the tarragon limps on until December so there are always a few sprigs for a bottle of vinegar. My French vinegar contains a bay leaf, a peeled shallot, and a sprig of thyme; the Italian garden vinegar has Italian parsley in it as well as a peeled garlic clove and a leaf of basil if there is one. The luxuriant basil crop, which seemed endless in August, has withered and gone starting with the cool September evenings. The leaves may be withered and yellowed, but tucked away in the freezer are some pots of pesto and basil oil ice cubes.

While rummaging through the Keats section of my *Oxford Quotations,* I actually came across a basil reference, which when quoted out of context suits this time of year and having to face the loss of basil:

For cruel 'tis, said she
To steal my Basil pot
away from me.

In fact, this poem is a gory murder story, but I will not delve into it as it would spoil the mellow fall atmosphere.

The swallow nests in the barn are all empty and their tenants gone till next spring. And the Canada geese that fly up the valley every morning and return to the sea at night are getting noisier; perhaps there is an edge of hunger in their raucous call. The three baby peacocks are as big as chickens and we hope they survive the winter and don't get nabbed by a voracious raccoon who in the past has performed a sort of population control for our flock.

October is a mellow month of bittersweet pleasures and endings. We turn from the garden and do more wintry things like walking, reading, writing, and cooking garlic- and onion-laced stews and roasts, glad of seasonal change that brings losses and appreciation for what will hopefully return in the spring. This is a good time for reflection and thankfulness because, in Keats's words: "Autumn and Nature have conspired to load and bless us with a bountiful harvest."

Fried Green Tomatoes with Cornmeal

The crunch of the green tomatoes and the rough texture of the cornmeal coating give new life to extra tomatoes lingering around the kitchen in October. Serve them with bacon, sausages, and eggs for a weekend fry-up, as a vegetable side dish with barbecued meats, or as a lunch dish with scrambled eggs. Ripe tomatoes may be used too, or mix them and have a red and green medley.

To make: Slice green tomatoes fairly thickly. Sprinkle with salt and pepper. Have a plate of cornmeal ready and press both sides of the slices firmly into the cornmeal. Sauté until crisp and golden in olive oil or butter—a few minutes a side. Serve on a warm platter and sprinkle with chopped parsley, chives, or green onion tops.

Green Tomato Pie

A friend brought this to a Thanksgiving potluck one year and it won more mmmms than the pumpkin pie. This is a Mennonite recipe adapted from Edna Staebler's *Food That Really Schmecks,* a Canadian culinary classic.

> Pastry for one 9-inch (23-cm) crust with a lid
> 3 cups (750 mL) green tomatoes
> 2 Tbsp. (30 mL) flour
> 3/4 cup (175 mL) brown sugar
> 1 tsp. (5 mL) cinnamon
> 1/4 tsp. (1 mL) nutmeg
> 1/2 cup (125 mL) molasses
> 1/4 cup (60 mL) water

Remove the stem end of the tomatoes, but don't peel them. Slice the tomatoes in thin rings, cover them with boiling water, and let stand for about 10 minutes, then drain them. Arrange them in the unbaked pie shell. Combine the flour, sugar, spices, molasses, and water. Pour the mixture over the tomato slices and cover with the top crust. Bake at 425°F (220°C) for 15 minutes and then at 350°F (180°C) for 30 more minutes. Serve with vanilla ice cream, whipped cream, or sweetened sour cream. Serves 8.

Green Tomato Marmalade

4 qt. (4 L) of green tomatoes, not skinned
12 cups (3 L) of sugar
2 lemons, sliced thin and diced fine
1/2 lb. (225 g) citron cut into small pieces

Cut the tomatoes into small pieces, cover with boiling water and cook for 5 minutes. Drain off the water. Put the tomatoes in a large pot with the sugar, lemons, and citron. Boil together for 1 1/2 hours, stirring frequently. When thick, pour into sterilized glasses and seal. This is an old prairie recipe; it makes a lovely Christmas gift with a batch of fresh biscuits.

Pumpkin Soup and Homemade Croutons

This recipe comes from my book *Winter Pleasures: Preserving and Cooking Herbs*. Pumpkins and squash decorate my kitchen from harvest time through the winter, until I have made the last one into soup, pie, or a decorative container for chili. The brilliant glow of orange on a gray winter day gladdens the cook's heart. This pumpkin soup is smooth, creamy, and delicate and is perked up with chopped herbs, croutons, and cheese.

4 cups (1 L) cooked pumpkin purée
4 cups (1 L) light cream or milk
1 tsp. (5 mL) sugar
Dash of salt
Freshly ground pepper
Sprinkle of nutmeg
2 cups (500 mL) of homemade croutons (recipe follows)
1/2 cup (125 mL) of chopped herbs (parsley, chives, or green onions)
1/2 cup (125 mL) grated Swiss or Parmesan cheese

You can use canned or frozen pumpkin in this recipe. If you are cooking your pumpkin from scratch, cut it in half or in quarters. Scoop out the seeds and stringy bits. Wrap in aluminum foil and place on a baking pan. Bake at 400°F (200°C) for about one hour, until soft. Scoop the cooked pumpkin out of the shell and purée in the food processor.

To make the soup: Place the puréed pumpkin in a large saucepan.

Whisk in the cream or milk, sugar, salt, pepper, and nutmeg. Simmer slowly for about 15 minutes. Soup should be just about bubbling. Pour into warmed bowls and sprinkle with croutons, chopped herbs, and grated cheese. Serves 6.

Homemade Croutons

4-6 slices of bread, cubed

4 Tbsp. (60 mL) olive oil

1 clove of garlic peeled and chopped

Sauté the cubed bread in the olive oil. Add the garlic. Stir well until croutons are crisp and brown. Place on paper toweling to soak up excess oil.

Hope End Hotel

firmly believe that if I receive four or five messages about a subject I should pursue it. My first message about Hope End Hotel came in the form of a novel by Margaret Forster called *A Lady's Maid*. The novel was written through the eyes of Elizabeth Barrett Browning's maid, and Hope End was mentioned as Barrett's childhood home where she lived for twenty-three years. Next, a magazine editor visiting our farm suggested we visit Hope End Hotel because it had a beautiful eighteenth-century walled vegetable garden where a vast array of fruits and vegetables are organically grown for the hotel table.

A month later, I picked up a copy of a magazine and there again was Hope End Hotel. Photographs displayed exquisite, dreamy scenes of the garden and oriental minarets from the remains of the old house. The article told the story of a barrister and a literature teacher who had taken their passion for organic gardening and true regional cooking and created Hope End Hotel.

The 1993 *Good Food Guide* published by Hodder & Stoughton describes the garden as "revivalist," a sanctuary for forgotten vegetables such as sea kale, sorrel, lovage, and cardoons. The guide says that the garden rules the menu and that herbs, fruit relishes, and preserves dictate the flavor of the food.

We made a trip to Hertfordshire, England, in the fall several years ago and Hope End was first on our list of places to visit. As we arrived we drove past apple orchards and rows of hop vines in the mellow October sunshine. Down the long driveway to Hope End one could see the minarets and ruined walls that frame the restored hotel. One of the owners, John Hegarty, greeted us while rolling a wheelbarrow of vegetables to the kitchen. We were soon ensconced in a comfortable room with views over the old courtyard. I immediately searched out the walled garden, which was a brief walk up the hill above the house. I opened a door to the garden and stepped into a Merchant-Ivory movie. There were arched doorways and restored white-trimmed greenhouses sheltering such exotics as lemons, jasmine, and basil. Fruit trees were carefully espaliered against the brick walls, and in the center were rows of beautiful vegetables—artichokes, asparagus, cabbages, spinach—and many kinds of fruit bushes.

Large clay pots to force sea kale and rhubarb were stacked against the wall, and forty kinds of apple trees lined one end of the garden. One expected to see Beatrix Potter painting in one corner and Mr. McGregor chasing Peter through the lettuces. I felt a wonderful sense of peace and tranquility, which happens in garden landscapes cultivated in a profoundly traditional and organic way. There were no jarring notes, no tractor or heaped sacks of chemical fertilizer.

Dinner that evening in the candle-lit dining room featured Jerusalem artichoke and fennel soup, roast pork with quince, and a potato gratin. The flavors were clear and earthy. I tasted the freshness and knew the vegetables and fruits had not been bouncing about in trucks from France for days or weeks.

Patricia Hegarty, though her cooking is underpinned by the classic French style, feels very strongly about cooking English food.

She writes in the introduction to her cookbook *An English Flavour,* "A countryside groaning in abundance of luscious goodies—what need have we of French produce."

Jane Grigson, the English food writer and Patricia Hegarty's mentor and guru, wrote in her foreword to the book that Patricia is a rare bird among English food professionals. She is a regional cook working in Herefordshire where she has lived all of her life. In fact, her family has been there for six centuries, many of them connected with the land and producing food such as fruit, jam, and vinegar. This kind of rootedness to a piece of earth gives tastes and flavors usually found only in rural France and Italy.

Hope End Hotel, in existence for about a dozen years, is an immense amount of work and struggle. Finding suitable staff is difficult, but Patricia now has a young Frenchman who, ironically, she is teaching to cook in the English style.

She has fears about centralized food inspection by the European Common Market and how this might affect the taste and quality of food produced locally. She preserves chutneys and freezes fruit, practices that might be severely restricted in the future. A typical breakfast, for instance, included homemade bread, butter from Somerset, free-range eggs with bright yellow yolks, and homemade jams.

The hotel has three comfortable lounges simply furnished with large leather couches and beautiful paintings of idyllic garden landscapes by Crispin T. Jones. There is a slight severity to Hope End's decorating. It was a relief from many of the country hotels I have stayed at in England, which are so antiquated, beribboned, and chintzed that they make me nervous. I found the simplicity and serenity of the hotel's interiors quite captivating.

Patricia and her husband, John, have created at Hope End the bucolic fantasy many of us carry in our minds as we lead frantic urban lives. And it is little wonder that the rootedness and historical continuity at Hope End Hotel are treasured by returning guests. I found the Hegartys inspiring. They are a symbol of hope and encouragement to aspiring cooks and gardeners everywhere. For more information, write them at Hope End, Ledbury, Herefordshire, HR8 1JQ. Telephone 053-13613.

The following recipes are taken from *An English Flavour* by Patricia Hegarty.

Tomato and Rosemary Soup

1 Tbsp. (15 mL) unsalted butter
1 medium onion, sliced
2 cups (500 mL) hot chicken stock
2 lbs. (900 g) ripe tomatoes
3 Tbsp. (45 mL) water
Sprig of fresh rosemary
Sea salt
Freshly ground black pepper

Melt the butter in a large saucepan over moderate heat and cook the onion until transparent, about 5 minutes. Add the chicken stock and cook for a further 10 minutes. Pour contents into the bowl of a food processor or blender, liquidize, and sieve.

Meanwhile, chop the tomatoes and place them in another saucepan with the water. Cook until soft, about 15 to 20 minutes. Remove from the heat, push through a sieve, and stir the tomato purée into the stock. Simmer with the rosemary for 10 minutes. Season and serve hot, garnished with a grinding of black pepper. Serves 6.

Roast Pork and Quince

3 lbs. (1.5 kg) boneless loin of pork with skin intact
Sea salt
2 quinces
1 cup (250 mL) pear cider (approximately)
1 Tbsp. (15 mL) whole cloves
Liquid honey
12 black peppercorns, crushed
3 Tbsp. (45 mL) whole wheat breadcrumbs
1 Tbsp. (15 mL) whole wheat flour
Quince jelly, to serve

Remove the skin from the pork by cutting through the fat, leaving half attached to the meat in an even layer. Score the fat by cutting deep slashes into it and rub all over with sea salt. Put into a shallow roasting pan, fat side down, and reserve the skin for crackling.

Peel, slice, and core the quinces. Put into a saucepan with a little cider over a gentle heat and cook until tender. Strain and reserve the cooking juices.

Preheat oven to 400°F (200°C). Lay the quinces over the inside of the joint, scatter with a few cloves, and close the sides together, securing the roll with wooden skewers or kitchen string tied at intervals along the joint.

Smear honey all over the fat. Mix together the crushed peppercorns and breadcrumbs and press evenly over the honeyed fat. Dot with more cloves. Pour a 1/2 cup (125 mL) of the reserved quince cooking juices into the roasting pan, cover with aluminum foil, and roast for 1 3/4 hours or until the juices run clear when pierced with a sharp knife.

Twenty minutes before the cooking time is up, remove the foil and put the skin on a baking sheet on the highest shelf of the oven above the pork.

When the pork is cooked, remove from the oven and leave to settle for a few minutes before carving. Watch the crackling carefully and remove it when it is crisp and brittle. Keep warm.

Just before serving, carve the pork into thin slices. Spoon off most of the fat from the roasting pan and sprinkle in the flour. Mix well. Add any additional quince cooking juice and enough cider to make 1 cup (250 mL) of gravy.

Serve the quince-stuffed pork with pieces of crackling, soufflé potatoes, and brussels sprouts. Hand round the gravy and quince jelly separately. Serves 6.

Viva Las Veggies

My first visit to Italy was a honeymoon in Venice and I do not remember the vegetables I ate, so overwhelmed was I by the art, the architecture, and the whole sensual ambience. Each night at 6 P.M. a gondolier would glide by my hotel window, which jutted out over the canal. He always sang and I began to wave to him every evening to thank him for his contribution to my Venetian experience.

Several years later, I returned to Italy where we drove through Tuscany in mellow October sunshine. The names of the towns connect like a necklace of memories—Orvieto, Florence, Siena, Perugia, Assisi, Urbino, and San Gimignano—and I do remember the vegetables I ate. We had arrived at the time of the porcini mushroom harvest. Along the sides of the country roads old ladies and young children were selling baskets of these delicious fungi. They hung by strings from houses, drying for the winter, and wherever we ate we were served porcini, marinated, sautéed, or baked for lunch and dinner. Their pungent, meaty, earthy taste has never left my memory.

Sadly, we cannot grow porcini in our vegetable garden. But other Italian vegetables will grow in a coastal garden and will add a taste of Italy to your dinners.

Of course, technically, there is no such thing as an Italian vegetable; the same veggies are grown and cooked all over the world. But there is definitely an Italian style in cooking *verdura*, the Italian word for vegetable.

Viana La Place, the California chef and cookbook writer, states in her wonderful book *Verdura, Vegetables Italian Style:* "Verdura is a word that at its root means green, and which conjures up images of green fields, freshness and the natural world. To me, verdura represents a style of eating directly related to nature, with vegetable at the centre."

La Place continues in her preface, saying that Italians have enormous respect for vegetables, which they consider part of the fabric of Italian life.

Marcella Hazan is my other favorite Italian cookbook writer, and she has inspired me to cook vegetables Italian-style. Her two volumes, *The Classic Italian Cookbook* and *More Classic Italian Cooking* plus *Marcella's Kitchen* are books that I might take to a desert island—if only to read and dream about for I might have only coconuts, seaweed, and fish to cook. Several friends have taken classes from Marcella and I have questioned them closely. What is my heroine like? They have informed me she is sometimes crabby, she smokes, and she once burst into tears in a class but was quickly comforted by her husband, Victor. Despite her volatile emotions, they found her culinary classes delicious and inspirational.

Marcella's books inspired me to search for arugula seeds so we could grow that spicy, peanutty, bitter green. Twelve years ago it was not easy to find, but I tracked some down in Seattle at a garden shop near Pike Place Market. I also discovered Angelo M. Pellegrini, a Seattle English professor whose books *The Food Lover's Garden* and *The Unprejudiced Palate* would incite anyone to dig up his or her backyard and plant verdura. The arugula seeds were duly planted and we discovered that if you are careful and let your arugula go to seed, you will have continuous arugula with short waits for germination and growing. This self-sowing plant reproduces with ease and generosity and with luck you may never have to buy seeds again. The bitter, pungent flavor gives humdrum salads zing.

Although considered an upmarket trendy green in North America, in Italy arugula grows wild and people gather it in vacant lots and fields and regard it as a peasant salad green.

Once, when I was suffering from a dreadful flu virus, Andrew made me *zuppa dei poveri con la rucola* from Marcella's second volume, which translated means poor man's soup and consists of potatoes, bread, arugula, water, and a touch of olive oil. It tasted so comforting and nourishing with the contrast between the bland potato and the sharp green that I decided life was worth living if soups such as this existed.

The vegetable fennel, *finocchio* in Italian, is one of my favorites and it also grows well on the B.C. coast. It likes to grow in the cool weather so it is planted in late July and bulbs up in the cooler fall. Raw, steamed, boiled, sautéed, or baked, it is a versatile anise-flavored vegetable like a licorice celery. Stores often misname it and call it anise. Italians think it is very good for the digestion and serve it at the end of a meal, which provides a crisp, clean crunch for the palate after a rich meal. The perennial herb fennel looks the same as the annual vegetable but does not have the above-ground bulb. If you plant it in the spring, it probably won't bulb up as the weather will have become too warm.

I love it chopped and raw dressed with my best olive oil. It is a great addition to an antipasto platter or served with a good blue cheese at the end of dinner (quite delicious with English Stilton). My quickest recipe is to blanch the chopped fennel, drain it, cover it with fresh grated Parmesan, and then slip it under the broiler until it is golden and bubbly and the cheese has formed a delicious crust. This is a very adaptable Marcella recipe that I use for many other vegetables, such as ribs of Swiss chard, asparagus, endive, and zucchini. Fennel also makes a delicate, delectable soup with the tantalizing zing of anise.

Swiss chard is another vegetable Italians cook with originality. It will cheerfully stand in a coastal winter garden waiting patiently for the cook. The ribs are most often used, and after a brief cooking in boiling water they can be drained, then dressed with olive oil, lemon juice, and pepper for an unusual, refreshing salad.

Fava beans, or broad beans as the English call them, are another Italian favorite. They are like a large, meaty lima bean and when picked young are delicious raw. The skins contain a faint, bitter taste and when older the skins can be removed after cooking. They are good in soups and stews or simply puréed. In a coastal garden, they can be planted in October or November along with the garlic and peas.

Other vegetables loved by the Italians are artichokes, which when given rich soil and lots of water will not only provide you with a delicious vegetable but will contribute a gigantic, silver, architectural plant to your garden. The artichoke's cousin, the cardoon, which looks like a huge, silver Scottish thistle, is also an interesting perennial vegetable. It is the ribs of the leaves, not the thistle, that are eaten. Both these plants look very attractive at the back of a flower bed. Cardoon ribs are blanched like the ribs of Swiss chard.

Purple, sprouting broccoli has a patch of its own in the garden and winters over, providing crunchy florets in March and April when we are dying for a fresh new vegetable.

With the addition of peppers, eggplants, Roma tomatoes, garlic, basil, oregano, sage, and a bay tree, one can have all the ingredients for an Italian garden transplanted to British Columbia. Just make sure you have the corresponding ingredients in your kitchen: a bottle of olive oil, a large chunk of Parmesan cheese, and Marcella Hazan's books.

Buon appetito! I will close by quoting Marcella again: "Eating in Italy is one more manifestation of the Italian age-old gift of making art out of life."

Growing Italian Vegetables

FENNEL

Fennel has a number of names and even the seed catalogs are contradictory. The herb fennel is perennial and does not bulb at the base. The vegetable fennel, normally called Florence, is annual or biennial, produces a sweet and tasty bulb at ground level, and is easy to grow in coastal areas of B.C.

Sowing time is critical; I swear by July 18, but any time between July 10 and 25 should be satisfactory.

First dig a shallow trench, fork in old manure or compost with added nitrogen, and partially fill in trench to within 3 inches (7.5 cm) of soil surface. Sow 2 or 3 seeds every 8 inches (20 cm). Water daily in dry weather until an inch or two high then thin the seedlings to 1 every 8 inches (20 cm).

The bulbs will start to form in September; the row should then be top-dressed with compost or fertilizers and should be watered daily if your soil drains quickly. The bulbs should be kept covered with soil as they increase in size and can be harvested at fist size or larger in October or November. You may have to phone around for seeds. Try Richters, Shepherds, Suttons, or Territorial.

ARUGULA, RUCOLA, ROCKET
This nutty-flavored Brassica relative is easily grown for its leaves. It can be sown in late spring and again in late summer. A 4-foot (1.2-m) row can supply a family. Late spring and summer sowings are best under Reemay, which provides ideal growing conditions in hot weather and keeps out flea beetles. The soil needs to be well supplied with nitrogen and watered every day if your soil drains quickly. In coastal British Columbia, September sowings will last most of the winter if protected by a cold frame. Leave a few plants to flower. The flowers are edible and the seeds are easily collected for future sowings. Richters and Shepherds carry the seeds.

FAVA BEANS
In coastal B.C., this overwintering crop is best sown in late October to mid-November, but I have had success sowing in unfertilized ground as late as December 5. A severe winter will kill the plants and the row can be resown in late January or February. Plants will benefit from a feeding with fish fertilizer in late February. Overwintered beans are sometimes less troubled with black fly, but young flowering shoots should be nipped off as soon as the black fly appears in April or May. 'Aquadulce' is a good overwintering variety. 'Windsor Long Pod' is good for early spring plantings.

—Andrew Yeoman

True, Stew Winter Pleasures

November is a month that tests the resilience of one's character. There is no deluding oneself that there will be more golden days of Indian summer. If you bravely turn and face reality, you know that ahead of you are gray, rainy days, and dark early evenings.

It is time to draw in and nest, to rely on those dependable and true pleasures of winter such as fires, books, candlelight, music, the company of good friends and, of course, good robust comfort food that makes one feel safe, nourished, and nurtured.

The vegetable garden has begun to look a little gloomy and moldy but there are still productive corners where, in my proper gleaning costume (green wellies and a long Aussie oiled raincoat), I have ventured out to find some treasures to cook and eat. I believe in props and costumes for gardening and most other activities. I love my English trug, special clippers, and long dramatic raincoat. Basic activities of life can be intensified by the right props and costumes, be they striped butcher aprons from England or a French peasant's navy blue cotton smock to wear for gathering eggs.

In the summer months, Andrew lets many plants hang around and go to seed. It looks like a wild desert at the end of August, but with the September rain there is a transformation and a great flush of new seedlings, such as Russian kale, small, tender, and perfect in salads, soups, or stir-fries, or Japanese red mustard, which has an astringent Dijon bite that adds new life to pale lettuces and miso soup. I make arugula salads—nothing but the distinctive spiciness of the arugula dressed with olive oil, lemon juice, and pepper. It is a great pleasure to harvest these self-sown greens, and as I fill my basket I give thanks to these generous plants.

Some planting goes on in November. Garlic, shallots, green peas, and broad beans can all be planted if you have not done so in October (see "November's Kitchen Garden," which follows). A trench of sweet peas can also be planted and you will have a head start in the spring. The Belgian endive is also clipped and covered and sent on to its next state. In the spring we will have a few weeks with a surfeit of endive to eat raw or cooked.

We stage a Christmas craft fair in the barn every November and light the woodstove, clean the barn, and deck it with boughs and lights. Local artists bring their treasures to sell, and the sheep and donkey are put in the manger. The aroma of hot apple cider permeates the barn, and we play Christmas carols. Flocks of people come to share in this piece of country theater and they enjoy taking part in it as much as we enjoy putting it on. Events like this brighten up a gray November.

The animals are quieter in November. Alex the peacock, whose tail feathers fell out in July, is still moping around, regretting the loss of his trailing glory, though by Christmas he will have grown a new fan of feathers and will be strutting his stuff again. The ewes are pregnant and seem only to be focused on eating, and the new hens of summer are now laying big brown eggs. Their first attempts at egg laying are tiny pullet eggs, which are so charming in a basket of straw I hate to eat them.

I love being in the tinned-roof barn when the November rain

starts to pelt down. Sitting on a bale of hay listening to the rhythmic drumming of the rain can be a soothing moment in a busy day. I think of European peasants who in the past shared their houses with their animals. Soft, breathing, comforting presences. I come to fully understand this way of life as I sit in the barn and listen.

My cooking changes in November, no longer content with the flimsy tossed-off meals of summer. I long for rich winy beef stew flavored with bay and thyme, pot roasts surrounded by caramelized onions and garlic, and meatballs laced with sour cream. I want mashed potatoes and baked potatoes and squash soup. I use the stronger herbs for flavoring now—piny, resinous rosemary, salty sage, and piquant peppery winter savory. These strong rich flavors cut the fatty taste of meat and help combat the damp and winter dark. My taste in wines changes also to robust rugged reds and I see November also encourages my taste for alliteration.

November is the best month for dinner parties. Make a delicious stew, have good bread—invite your dearest friends and someone new. If the dearest friend says, "What can I bring?" pounce and say dessert and there, you are done. Set the table, light the fire and lots of candles and have a happy evening, for this will calm the existential angst and loneliness that often accompany November. Our cave ancestors did this when they lit the first fire in their caves on a blustery night and huddled together for comfort.

Winter vegetables are very beautiful, and I decorate the kitchen and table with red and green cabbages and pale yellow parsnips. Vegetables lead to soup, which can be a complete meal. Parsnip, potato, carrot, beets, and cabbage are my winter choices. Cook and then purée the vegetables and add some chicken stock and milk or cream. Voilà, la soupe. Cooked puréed vegetables freeze very well and are ready to throw into some hot stock.

Last month I quoted Keats because his lines about mists and mellow fruitfulness fit October so well. This month, another encounter of the poetic kind found me reading a haiku about this penultimate month. There is something about the simplicity of Japanese "one-breath poetry" that suits the season:

> *On a sunny November afternoon*
> *With a cold, eating a*
> *persimmon.*

Years ago I taught a Grade 7 class to write haiku, and I read and wrote so many the form is wedged in my brain. I occasionally write them to celebrate some small, happy event. The writing of this column inspired a stew haiku:

> *Rainy November night*
> *Light the candles*
> *The stew bubbles laced with bay leaves.*
> *Eat, my friends!*

So make that stew, light the candles, and be assured, the gloom of November will lift.

Beef Stew with Onions, Mushrooms, and Orange Rind

Using orange rind in meat dishes is very common in the south of France and adds a fillip to the taste. Sometimes I pop in some tiny frozen peas at the end. This dish is a complete meal in a pot, with a loaf of crusty bread to mop up the gravy. This recipe comes from *Winter Pleasures: Preserving and Cooking Herbs*.

2 lb. (900 g) stewing beef cut into cubes
4 Tbsp. (60 mL) flour—enough to dredge the meat
Freshly ground pepper
Dash of cayenne
4 Tbsp. (60 mL) vegetable oil
4 medium onions (red or yellow), thinly sliced
4-6 cloves garlic, peeled and minced
1 lb. (450 g) mushrooms, sliced
3-4 long strips of orange rind
6 carrots, peeled and sliced into rounds
1 cup (250 mL) beef stock, fresh or canned
1 cup (250 mL) dry red wine
3 bay leaves (preferably fresh as they have the most fragrance)

Preheat oven to 350°F (180°C). Toss beef cubes in a bag with flour, pepper, and cayenne until the cubes are well floured. Heat oil in a large fry pan and brown the cubes of beef on all sides. Remove meat to an ovenproof baking dish or a Dutch oven.

Sauté the onions, garlic, and mushrooms for a few minutes in the fry pan and add to the meat.

Add orange rind and sliced carrots to the pan. Pour the beef stock and red wine over the carrots and bring to a boil. Pour carrots, wine, and stock over the meat and vegetables. Add bay leaves and a little more ground black pepper. Cover and bake for 1 1/2 hours. Cook a little longer if needed. Add extra liquid if necessary. Remove bay leaves before serving. Serves 4-6.

Lake O'Hara Pear and Parsnip Soup

I once had an excellent pear parsnip soup at Lake O'Hara Lodge in the Rockies and they kindly gave me the recipe. The sweet fruity pear plus the earthy-tasting parsnip make a superb combination in your soup bowl.

5-6 parsnips, peeled and sliced
4 pears, cored and diced
1/2 onion diced
3-4 Tbsp. (45-60 mL) butter or olive oil
4 cups (1 L) vegetable or chicken stock
3 potatoes, peeled and diced
3/4 tsp. (4 mL) ground coriander
3/4 cup (175 mL) heavy cream
Salt and pepper
Cilantro leaves

Sauté parsnips, pears, and onions in butter or olive oil. Do not brown.

Add stock, potatoes, and coriander. Boil, then simmer until all ingredients are soft. Blend in a food processor. Return to heat and add cream. Season to taste with salt, pepper, and fresh cilantro leaves. Serves 4.

November's Kitchen Garden

In coastal B.C. garden gamblers can sow peas and broad beans now. The odds are better than a penny mining stock and you can eat the results and not pay weight gain tax. You might want to experiment in your own garden.

Choose early maturing varieties like 'Little Marvel' (pea) and 'Aquadulce' or 'Windsor Long Pod' (broad beans).

The bed should have good drainage; a little bonemeal should be forked in before sowing, and the plants will benefit from some liquid fish fertilizer in late February. Harvesting begins in May about 3 weeks before an early spring sowing.

The first days of November are the last planting days for garlic cloves if you want large-size bulbs in July. Plant the cloves base down just below the surface of the soil, 6 inches (15 cm) apart. The soil should be enriched with compost or fertilizer as well as organic matter; good drainage is essential.

November is also the month for cutting back the Belgian endive leaves at Ravenhill Farm. After cutting off the leaves 1/2 inch (1 cm) above the roots, there are two ways of growing the pale yellow-green chicons. Mine, the lazy person's way, is to cover the roots with 6 inches (15 cm) of untreated sawdust (not cedar) and harvest the chicons in late February, March, and April. My neighbor, Georges Rostoker, digs his roots up, shortens them to 8 inches (20 cm) long, and packs them vertically with a little peat moss in large plastic bucket. He then stores them in a dark cold cellar. Three weeks before harvesting the bucket is fertilized with liquid 20-20-20 and brought into a room-temperature dark room. This method extends the enjoyment of these culinary treasures from late November to March or even April.

—Andrew Yeoman

The Little French Snob

es, there is a class structure in the onion family, and at the very top is the refined, discreet, aristocratic shallot. Small and elegant, it has a finer, more subtle flavor than that of the common onion. The flesh has a tighter texture and is crisper and less watery, which is why recipes for the classic sauces of haute cuisine demand shallots, not onions.

Shallots have other culinary advantages: they are very tender, they are delicious but not overpowering when eaten raw, and they cook very quickly when chopped or minced.

In the sixties, when I was in my graduate-student cooking stage (meat loaf and spaghetti sauce), I never used shallots—partly because of my culinary ignorance and partly because they were almost impossible to find. A decade or so later, after falling under Julia Child's spell and traveling to France, I developed an attachment to these mauve-pink members of the onion family. Their faint sweetness and whiff of garlic had seduced me.

The first year at our herb farm, a friend from Vernon who was a stockbroker-turned-shallot-grower mailed us a pound of shallot bulbs, with instructions not to sell shallots in his area of the province. We readily agreed to this demand and Andrew carefully planted the bulbs that fall. Eagerly we awaited the following summer's rich bounty, for the shallot is the most generous of bulbs—plant one and find eight in its place. A French neighbor,

Georges, who is a wonderful vegetable gardener, gave us some exotic varieties, gray shallots and shallots shaped like chicken thighs called *cuisse de poulet*.

That summer I began my ongoing course in shallot cookery. I searched through cookbooks and found many ways to include these crisp little morsels in our meals. Here are some suggestions for how you can use your shallot harvest if you are a cook-gardener. If you don't grow your own shallots, haunt the markets and buy a stash when they appear crisp and new in the summer and fall.

- ❀ I love to roast them, peeled and whole, alongside a leg of lamb or a roast of beef. They will be juicy and fragrant and will flavor your pan gravy in a wonderful way.

- ❀ Add them finely minced to a vinaigrette dressing. Or, for dressing, marinades, or sauces, add some chopped shallots to red or white wine vinegar and let steep.

- ❀ Peel a large amount of shallots (quantity depends on your patience or the amount of kitchen slave labor you have coerced). Freeze them whole in a screw-top jar and then take them out as you need them, quickly returning the bottle to the freezer.

- ❀ Sprinkle a finely minced shallot on raw sliced tomatoes with freshly ground pepper and olive oil. A plain butter lettuce salad cries out for a sprinkle of raw chopped shallots.

- ❀ To raise a beef stew to new heights, peel about twelve whole shallots and add them along with the other vegetables.

- ❀ Sauté some minced shallots in olive oil and sprinkle them on a homemade pizza (or a delivered one). Add a 1/2 cup (125 mL) of sautéed, minced shallots to a recipe for French bread or quick biscuits—bread and members of the onion family are good companions.

If you have never grown any shallots before and have garden space, do try your hand at it. Shallots are very rewarding and are easier to grow than regular onions. My campaign is to encourage more people to grow shallots so they will become as common as regular onions. The price will come down and once democratized, the little French snob will turn into a regular staple. Vive la révolution! Let them eat shallots.

Roast Beef Sandwiches with Shallot and Red Wine Butter

This is a great way to use up both the meat and the heels of the wine bottles left over from a roast beef dinner.

Sliced French bread or French rolls split open
Shallot and Red Wine Butter (recipe follows)
Several slices of cold cooked roast beef
Freshly cracked black pepper

Spread French bread or rolls with shallot and red wine butter. Add roast beef slices and sprinkle with pepper.

Shallot and Red Wine Butter

1 Tbsp. (15 mL) olive oil
2 shallots, finely chopped
1 cup (250 mL) red wine
1 cup (250 mL) butter, at room temperature

Heat the oil in a small saucepan and add the shallots. Sauté the shallots until just softened. Add the red wine and simmer until the mixture has reduced in volume to 1/4 cup (60 mL). Remove from the heat and let cool completely. Mix the red wine/shallot mixture with the butter and place in the refrigerator to firm up slightly. Butter will be a rosy pink color. Makes 1 cup (250 mL).

Easy Shallot Pickles

I adapted this from *The Greens Cookbook* by Deborah Madison and Edward Espe Brown. They are quick to make and delicious with sandwiches. They keep for a week covered in the refrigerator.

1 lb. (450 g) shallots
1 qt. (1 L) boiling water
2/3 cup (150 mL) rice wine vinegar
2/3 cup (150 mL) cold water
10 black peppercorns
2-3 bay leaves

Peel the shallots and slice them into thin rounds. Separate the rings and put them in a colander. Pour boiling water over the sliced shallots. Add the rice wine vinegar, cold water, peppercorns, and bay leaves. Cover and refrigerate 1 hour before serving.

Shallot-Cream Herbed Pasta Sauce

A really delicious quickie. Use whatever herbs are in the garden.

2 cups (500 mL) light cream
2 shallots, minced
4 Tbsp. (60 mL) mixed chopped herbs: chives, parsley, oregano, etc.
Freshly ground pepper and salt to taste

Heat the cream with the shallots and herbs. Boil almost a minute, or until the sauce is as thick as you like it. Grind in some pepper, and serve over cooked pasta with a bowl of freshly grated Parmesan cheese. Sprinkle some fresh chopped chives on top. Serves 4.

The Shallot

Like most of the onion family, shallots require a rich to moderately rich fast-draining soil. Bulbs can be planted in October, or April in cooler climates, 4 inches (10 cm) apart, with the tips just showing above the soil. Many nurseries now carry shallots, but you have to be careful with store-bought ones, which may have been dosed with a growth inhibitor for long storage. I've planted some grocery-bought shallots in October and pulled them out in March still vital and alive but without any top growth.

Like garlic, shallots benefit from 2 applications of nitrogen-rich fertilizer (fish fertilizer or blood meal) in late February and early to mid-March. Shallots should be watered in dry periods from March to the end of May and should not be watered in June and July.

Harvesting is normally in mid to late July when the tops turn yellow. Pull the shallots, expose the roots to the sun for a day or 2 and then dry them on racks. After cleaning and separating the roots, store them in net bags in a cool, dry place with good air circulation.

—Andrew Yeoman

The Stinking Rose

hoosing books and music for a prolonged stay on a desert island has been turned into a new game for cooks. What would you take to flavor the food? The salt shaker? The pepper grinder? A large jar of Dijon or a string of garlic? The garlic would be my immediate choice. I would put strings around my neck and stuff my pockets hoping I could plant some on the island and be a self-sufficient cook Friday.

Food historians trace garlic back to Asia, and for centuries garlic has been performing magic on the simplest ingredients such as beans, rice, bread, and pasta. It is a democratic herb that generously flavors the food of a Mexican farmer or a French king. It can turn basic foods into masterpieces. Garlic has a multilayered hot and peppery flavor when raw, and when cooked slowly in liquid it gains a mellow sweetness. The rough edges smooth out, adding a complex, rich taste to dishes that is usually equaled only by adding meat stock. Garlic cooked whole and slowly acquires a meaty puréed texture that is delicious in lamb, chicken, or bean dishes.

Cooking methods for garlic can vary. Many cookbooks warn one not to cook minced garlic at a high heat, and from years of experience I have found this to be true. Once it gets brown it develops an acrid flavor. There is also controversy over garlic presses. Purists dislike them and report that presses also release the garlic's bitter juices. I prefer to use a knife for crushing and mincing. Microwaves don't improve garlic's flavor either.

On my last visit to San Francisco, I made my annual pilgrimage to the City Lights bookstore but I got sidetracked into an early lunch by the smell wafting from a restaurant called vividly The Stinking Rose. The menu had cute little drawings of garlic cloves flirting with chickens, folk dancing with potatoes, and chasing vampires down the street. And it was there that I had the best garlic-laced lunch of my life. On each table was a glass jar of fresh parsley pesto full of garlic and Parmesan cheese. The pesto was for slathering on hot French bread, pasta, and chips, or dolloping on our soup. I had a rich bean soup with whole garlic cloves and a superb Caesar salad with whole romaine leaves, minced fresh garlic, garlicky croutons, and large shavings of fresh Parmesan.

This subject brings up the sometimes taboo subject of the dreaded garlic breath. And if you are the sort of person who worries about such things, a chaser of fresh parsley after a garlicky meal is supposed to help. Being of Anglo-Saxon background, I never saw a clove of garlic until the late fifties. Deep in my heart I had always known that somewhere out there, there was food with more taste than my mother's over-boiled and over-roasted dinners. My first taste of garlic confirmed this unequivocally. Shortly after I cooked my first garlic dinner. I put it in the vinaigrette, rubbed the salad bowl with a cut clove, rubbed the Sunday roast beast with another cut clove, minced some into the Oxo gravy and made hot garlic bread. My papa mildly suggested that I might have gone over the top, but they were encouraging parents and were patient with my early culinary forays.

Though the aromatic history of garlic is vague, some feel that the Romans brought it to England as the Roman army fed it to its soldiers daily for health and courage. For some reason garlic fell out of favor with British cooks in the sixteenth century. By the nineteenth century Mrs. Beeton hardly mentions it. An older generation of WASPs titters about garlic as if they were discussing sex. No garlic please, we're British. But one very positive thing about the baby boomer generation is that they have wholeheartedly accepted garlic as an essential part of life. North American restaurants will never be the same—thank goodness.

Garlic is harvested in summer and should be stored to cure and dry in an airy space. I have ours in net bags in the garage or barn. Do not refrigerate or keep in a too-warm kitchen. Do not substitute with garlic salt or garlic powder. One of the more disgusting culinary calamities of the sixties was garlic bread made with garlic salt.

If you are peeling a lot of cloves (tedious work, but necessary for such dishes as chicken with forty cloves of garlic), pour a glass of wine and sit down at a table to work. Play the Gipsy Kings for encouragement. I got this idea from a Spanish friend in his fifties who also ate raw garlic for breakfast. He had a young girlfriend and he said garlic helped virility. Actually, if you eat enough of it, garlic is supposed to improve just about everything, except your social life. I've even heard that tossing a clove into your dog's dish will keep ticks and fleas away. Ask your guests to peel garlic for you. It's the perfect answer to the feeble "Can I help?" question that hostesses often get. If you're left to do the job alone, pour boiling water over the cloves for two minutes. This loosens the skins so that they slip off easily.

Buy an organic supply in July or August and store. Suddenly, local organic garlic is being grown up and down the B.C. coast. I salute these garlic farmers. One farmer I met at the Vernon market (who looked thirtysomething) announced to all passersby that he was eighty-five and his youthful appearance was the result of a garlic-laced diet.

The B.C. coast is a perfect place to grow garlic. Andrew, the grower at our farm, has written some specific growing tips, which I have included. I have also included some simple but delicious recipes from my book *Winter Pleasures: Preserving and Cooking Herbs.* These recipes will give the cook and garlic lover the full glorious robust taste of the stinking rose.

For added safety insurance when I travel, I carry a few bulbs of garlic in my purse. It makes me feel secure—a culinary backup. I am ready to take on any vampires or even that desert island.

Bruschetta

If you have any leftover country-style bread, this is a divine way to use it up. In the purest circumstances, the bread should be grilled over a wood fire (a bistro in Seattle grills it over applewood), but it is very simple to make at home. Just toast sliced French bread under the broiler, on a barbecue, or in the toaster. Rub the toast with a peeled, cut, slightly crushed clove of garlic, sprinkle with pepper, and drizzle with olive oil. Serve immediately, while it is still hot.

Try topping the bruschetta with chopped cooked tomatoes after it is grilled. Drizzle the olive oil on top of the tomatoes. Serve with a glass of wine as a simple but delicious appetizer, or with soup and salad for a light meal.

Baked Garlic

Serve these garlic bulbs with a basket of hot French bread. Your dinner guests can squeeze the garlic cloves out of their papery shells and spread them onto the hot bread. With a glass of red wine, this makes a wonderful appetizer.

4 garlic bulbs or one per person
Olive oil

Preheat oven to 375°F (190°C). Leaving the garlic bulbs whole, snip away the untidy bits. Rub each bulb with olive oil. Place in a small baking dish and bake uncovered about 1 hour. The interior of the garlic will be smooth and creamy. Serves 4.

Aïoli Sauce

Aïoli is usually made at the farm in late July when the first garlic is harvested, but it is such amazing stuff that it should be made in winter. It is often called the butter of Provence, and villages have aïoli parties to celebrate the garlic harvest. Vegetables, fresh cod, shrimp, and French bread are dipped into this powerful sauce. I have served it on pasta, toasted French bread, barbecued meats, and every sort of vegetable, raw or cooked. Originally made with a mortar and pestle, it is now simple to make in a food processor. It has such flavor that it is truly a hymn to garlic.

8-12 garlic cloves, peeled
2 large egg yolks, at room temperature
Freshly ground pepper
Dash of salt
Juice of 1 lemon
1 tsp. (5 mL) Dijon mustard
1 1/2 cups (375 mL) olive oil

Purée the garlic in the food processor. Whisk the egg yolks in a small bowl until light and smooth, and add to the garlic in the processor. Add salt and pepper, lemon juice, and mustard to garlic and eggs. Process until smooth.

Slowly add the oil in a thin stream while the machine is running. Process until the sauce is thick, yellow, shiny, and firm. Refrigerate until ready to use.

For a basil-flavored variation, add 1 cup (250 mL) packed basil leaves to the garlic in the processor.

Serve the aïoli in a bowl on a large platter. Surround it with vegetables, seafood, or other favorite foods and have an aïoli party. Makes about 2 cups (500 mL).

Garlic Mashed Potatoes

In this dish, garlic adds new life to an old favorite. The powerful flavor of the garlic adds richness to the bland smoothness of the mashed potatoes. If there are any leftovers, you can form the potatoes into small cakes and sauté them.

4-6 cups (1-1.5 L) mashed potatoes
4 garlic cloves, peeled and left whole
1/2 cup (125 mL) chopped parsley (optional)
3 Tbsp. (45 mL) butter or margarine (optional)

Prepare your usual mashed potatoes. Set aside and keep warm. Place garlic in a saucepan of boiling water and simmer for 5 minutes, until soft. Remove from water and in a small bowl mash garlic with a fork until it is creamy. Add a bit of the garlic water to make the purée a little thinner. Add the garlic to the mashed potatoes and whip well with a masher. If desired, add chopped parsley, mix well, dot with butter or margarine and put under the broiler for a minute or so, until it is brown and bubbly. Serves 4-6.

The Garlic Year

The garlic year at Ravenhill Farm starts in October with the rituals of bed making, soil preparation, and planting. In southwest B.C., the garlic bed should have sun for more than half the day (preferably all day). The ground should drain well. In poorly drained soil, raised beds are essential. The soil should be rich in organic material and nutrients. Most local soils greatly benefit from the addition of lime and phosphorus in the form of bonemeal.

The larger outer cloves of the bulb are planted, pointed end up, about 6 inches (15 cm) apart and approximately 1 inch (2.5 cm) below the soil surface. Bulbs from the supermarket can be used but they are probably from California, so it is best to get garlic from your local market or a seed company, such as Salt Spring Seeds (P.O. Box 444, Ganges, Salt Spring Island, V8K 2W1).

The green tops should show in December or January, depending on soil temperature. In mid-February and again in early March, it is important to add nitrogen fertilizer to the cold soil. Fish fertilizers and blood meal are two good sources. In late March or early April, a source of potassium and phosphorus should be added—in the form of chicken manure, compost, or liquid seaweed. Ideally, the bed should be kept clean of competing weeds and the plants watered every 3 days in dry spells between March and mid-May.

After mid to late May the plants should not be watered. Harvesting begins when the tops turn yellow in early to mid-July. The bulbs are left to dry in the sun for a few hours before being placed in storage racks or hung up to dry for several weeks. After this, the dried tops can be cut off and the bulbs stored in small netted bags in a cool dry place with good air circulation.

—Andrew Yeoman

December Dreaming

ecember is a month best spent wishing, dreaming, and planning for the garden. Everything outside is standing still in the cold and gloom, but I am curled up in front of the fire reading garden books, garden magazines, and seed catalogs. One garden magazine from England called *Garden Illustrated* has given great pleasure to our lives. It is so visually beautiful and full of such wondrous articles on romantic gardens that it can make one feel quite faint with delight. I save every copy and keep them in a stack by the couch for low moments.

Magazines such as these make one dream of gazebos, and I make little drawings and plans for where I would place it—down by the vegetables or on the lawn looking over the valley? The pragmatic gardener I live with snorts at my gazebo dreaming and tells me to buy lottery tickets, though he thinks nothing of having $250 of well-rotted cow manure delivered.

As I sit warm and snug by the fire I dream of new gardens. A sushi chef we have known for years asked us one evening if we would grow the beefsteak plants called perilla (*shiso* in Japanese), which sushi chefs like to use in their creations. Perhaps, I think, from the comfort of my sofa, I will dig a long raised bed and fill it with perilla, which comes in green and red leaves. The new garden could also contain some shungiku, the edible chrysanthemum, Japanese onions, and various other greens. Our sushi chef insists there would be a big market for perilla as it cannot be bought from other suppliers. Perhaps next summer we will trade perilla for sushi. Bartering herbs and produce can be quite exciting, especially if you are trading with potters and other artists. Sometimes it takes a lot of basil to achieve one beautiful pot.

Catalog dreaming is another lovely way to spend a chilly December evening by the fire. Curl up with a glass of good port (I only drink it in December) and tick off your choices. One of my favorites is Shepherd Seeds from California, which each year produces a catalog full of pretty line drawings and a great collection of European seeds, basils, and flowers for drying as well as tools for cooking and gardening. Another favorite is *A Cook's Garden,* a wonderful source of salad greens, French and Italian vegetables, and basils. This is also a great source for arugula seeds, which can be hard to find. The *Cook's Garden* catalog is decorated with charming woodcuts of flowers and plants. Both companies will take fax orders, telephone orders, and credit cards. They will also accept old-fashioned mail-order letters.

With my gazebo and garden planned, I begin to think about decorating the house for Christmas. I go to our local nursery and buy pots and pots of red poinsettias and put them everywhere—in the kitchen, the bathroom, the guest rooms. I also love white cyclamen, and at night I put them in the cool porch so they will last longer. I buy white candles by the boxful, collect all my angel candle holders, and then go out and prune the giant cedars and bring in armloads of boughs. I always remember to thank the gentleman who planted the trees on our farm more than eighty years ago. I hope that in eighty years' time there will still be a farm here and someone will be cutting boughs and thanking us for planting trees for them to enjoy.

I deck the mantel with branches of cedar and holly, and put

pieces of holly behind the pictures just as my mother did. There is a tree farm next door to us and so we go and cut our own Christmas tree, an old-fashioned task that is certainly never a chore. Also down the road is a holly farm, and Robert the holly man makes beautiful wreaths. I buy one for the blue back door and one for the barn door. I think about these wonderful pagan customs of hanging greens and lighting candles at the darkest time of the year and how these customs have merged into a great anthropological muddle called Christmas. Having been an Anglican and a Catholic in my past, I now choose from an assortment of rituals and make my own muddle: angels, boughs, and the head of a Greek goddess (Hera, the goddess of health) on the mantel, surrounded by candles.

I become quite sentimental about the animals at Christmas and buy them red bows, toys, and indigestible treats. One year I put a huge red bow on Joker the donkey. He tore around the field wildly and chased the sheep--unused to having anything around his neck. The bow lasted for about a week before the goat pulled it off and chewed it. But before that happened I could look out the kitchen window and see Joker and this hit of Christmas red. I even thought of putting red bows on the six geese but decided that was a little over the top even for *Victoria* magazine, and besides, I can never get closer than ten feet to the geese before they start to hiss and come after me.

I get up early Christmas morning and do some gleaning in the garden. Tucked away in the cold frames I can still find parsley and sage leaves to slip under the turkey breast, which when roasted etches a pretty leaf formation under the golden skin (an idea I stole from Martha Stewart). I can usually find some Welsh onion, rosemary, and lemon thyme for the stuffing. In the greenhouse I pick some fresh bay leaves to flavor the bread sauce. My bay trees are planted in big Italian pots and get tucked away in the greenhouse from November until March. I put a small bay tree in the kitchen window for the winter for quick picking. Fresh bay in soup or a béchamel sauce fills your kitchen with its amazing scent. Put some leaves in a pot of water and simmer for a while for some real culinary theater. Bay trees in larger sizes are more readily available now than they were a few years ago. What a perfect present for a cook—a bay tree of generous proportion decorated with tiny kitchen utensils or gadgets.

Cooks and gardeners are lucky people at Christmas time. We are easy to buy for because there is such a surfeit of beautiful cookbooks and gardening books, and the specialty shops are full of tempting treasures like kitchen implements and various other devices. Buy a large pretty pot and fill it with some seeds for a balcony gardener. A serious composter would love some sacks of rotted horse manure (decorated with a large red ribbon, of course), which can usually be procured by driving out in the country where horsey types sell the product at the gate.

Take time in December to dream and make wishes and resolutions about next year's garden. I vow to plant more nasturtiums for my salads, to plant more lavender, to make the salad beds things of beauty with rows of red 'Lollo Rossa' lettuce and clumps of purple opal basil. One could make a design of an Oriental carpet with flowers and salad greens. The cooking of good food may be a temporary pleasure, but perhaps it is the thinking, the planning, the dreaming, and the wishing that are the most satisfying acts involving gardening and cooking. Joyeux Noël.

Christmas Chicken Liver Pâté

This is a rich-tasting pâté that I have been making for 20 years. I use shallots, for I like their sweetish, garlicky flavor, but onions will do.

1/2 lb. (225 g) chicken livers, membranes removed
1 cup (250 mL) chicken stock
1 bay leaf
1/2 cup (125 mL) chopped shallots or onions
2 Tbsp. (30 mL) butter or margarine
2 eggs, hard-cooked
Freshly ground pepper
A good dash of brandy

In a saucepan, simmer the livers in the chicken stock with the bay leaf for about 10 minutes. Drain and set aside, reserving the broth.

Sauté the shallots in the butter for 3 or 4 minutes or until the shallots are soft. Purée the livers and eggs in a food processor with a little of the reserved chicken stock to moisten. Add the shallots and process until well mixed. Add pepper and a dash of brandy. Process briefly. Serve the pâté in a crock with toast triangles and some sour pickles. Makes 2 cups (500 mL).

Christmas Mulled Apple Juice and Rum

Homemade apple juice mixed with rum, cloves, and cinnamon sticks and heated in my grandmother's huge copper jelly pan makes a wonderful drink for a Christmas party. The kitchen fills with steam and spicy smells, the windows fog up, and everyone has a wonderful time. The rum can be omitted and few will notice the difference.

4 qt. (4 L) apple juice
4 cups (1 L) dark navy rum
10 cinnamon sticks
20 cloves
2 lemons, thinly sliced
2 oranges, thinly sliced

Mix all ingredients in a large saucepan and heat. Leave simmering on the stove and let the guests help themselves.

Noël's Smoked Salmon Herb Dip and Spread

This pretty pale-pink dip flecked with green is something I make every Christmas. Serve it with hot French bread, crackers, or bagels. The herb varies depending on what I have on hand in the garden and in the freezer. Some Decembers, there is still chervil growing in the garden or I use frozen chives, dill, or fresh parsley and green onions.

8 oz. (225 g) of cream cheese
1/4 cup (60 mL) skim milk cottage cheese
1 Tbsp. (15 mL) lemon juice
1/2 cup (125 mL) chopped herb of your choice
2 shallots peeled and halved
4 oz. (115 g) smoked salmon (lox type)
Freshly ground pepper

Combine all ingredients in a food processor or blender and process until smooth and well mixed. Serve in a bowl with crackers or raw vegetables. Makes about 1 1/2 cups (375 mL).

Gifts from
a Gardener's Kitchen

 ong ago I had a friendship with a wealthy, eccentric old American lady. When she returned from her yearly sojourn in Paris she would shower me with perfume, Chanel beads, and designer scarves. I pondered long and hard over what I could give her in return, in appreciation. I finally gave her a pot of homemade raspberry jam and a small loaf of homemade brown bread. The gift reminded her of her childhood at a summer place in New York State and tears came to her eyes. I realized that the simple gift made by me had given her more pleasure than anything bought in a store.

So here it is December and I am planning some homegrown gifts for my friends. I wander around the slightly gloomy December garden and find little areas of green pleasure and produce amongst the general desolation and decay of a winter plot. The beets are still safely underground, under a quilt of sawdust. The leeks are lined up in their soldier rows, ready to march into the soup pot. Some carrots are left. Parsleys, both curly and Italian, produce a gay path of green. There are still a few sorrel leaves and the usual herbs that comfort me in the winter: rosemary, thyme, winter savory, and red and green sage.

In the garage, barn, and freezer are stored potatoes, onions, garlic, shallots, apples, and pears.

With the beets and leeks, I can make robust pots of borscht and vichyssoise. The soup can be put in a decorated plastic freezer container, tucked into a basket with a fresh loaf of bread and covered with a pretty tea towel. The lucky recipient can either freeze the soup or enjoy it immediately. The carrots can be pickled or made into carrot marmalade. The bunches of parsley can be processed into a zesty parsley-garlic pesto to put on French bread or pasta. The sorrel would make a lovely pale green mayonnaise, and combined with some smoked trout, salmon, or fresh cooked prawns, would make a wonderful hostess gift or an appetizer for a potluck supper. The herbs, tied in bundles with a jar of cranberry jelly, would give the Christmas cook a cheery lift and a few things less to worry about. Jellies made from sage, thyme, or rosemary are unusual and delicious—good as condiments with meat dishes, bastings for poultry, or toppings for muffins and scones.

I ramble through my stored supplies, seeking gift inspiration. I look at the onions hanging in their string bags and contemplate an onion jam with some shallots and garlic added. Onion jam takes a plain burger or lamb chop into new taste terrain; it makes me realize how much the English like plain food with lots of strong condiments to add a little gustatory zing.

Gazing at the apples I think of applesauce, apple tart, and apple chutney. The pears, lined up in rows, are waiting patiently to be eaten or submerged in brandy.

My larder makes me happy and secure and inspires a delicious hour of browsing through a stack of cookbooks. I find Helen Witty's *Fancy Pantry,* one of the most stimulating condiment cookbooks I have read. I also collect older cookbooks put out by women's institutes, churches, and schools—a great source for homemade gifts.

Packaging kitchen gifts is half the fun. I collect unusual baskets, pretty napkins, and tea towels, bows, raffia twine, unusual jars and bottles, interesting serving spoons, and little spreading knives. Making cards and personal labels is also fun and easy with some colored cards and a set of felt pens.

All these activities are part of being a domestic sensualist. Artistic creations from the kitchen are transient, but they bring edible and visual pleasure to the recipient and the creator. Merry Christmas and a pot of onion jam to you too.

Herb Jelly

You can use this as a master recipe for all your herb jellies. If using rosemary or sage, however, you should use less than stated in the following recipe as these two herbs have strong volatile oils. As you become more experienced with jelly making, you can change the recipe to suit your palate.

1-2 cups (250-500 mL) washed and chopped fresh herbs
1 1/4 cups (300 mL) boiling water
1/4 cup (60 mL) white wine vinegar
3 cups (750 mL) white sugar
2 Tbsp. (30 mL) fresh lemon juice
2-3 drops of food coloring (optional)
1/2 bottle of liquid pectin
Sprigs of fresh herbs (optional)

Put the chopped herbs in a saucepan and pour the boiling water over them. Let sit for 15-20 minutes. The herbs release more flavor if they are chopped and if they steep for at least 15 minutes.

Strain the herb liquid through a coffee filter or cheesecloth into another saucepan. Add the vinegar, sugar, and lemon juice and bring to a boil, stirring well to dissolve the sugar. Add food coloring if desired, and pectin. Stir constantly for 1 minute. Remove from the heat. Skim off foam and pour mixture into hot sterilized jars. Put a sprig of the herb in the jelly at this time if you wish. Seal the jars with paraffin wax or canning lids. Label and store. Makes 4 cups (1 L).

Rhubarb Chutney

Thick, rich, tart, and darkly spiced, this chutney is delicious with curry dishes and cold meats and helps make leftovers more interesting. December is a good month to do a freezer inventory. I usually find several bags of frozen chopped rhubarb and the house fills with wonderful spicy smells.

2 cups (500 mL) cider vinegar
2 lbs. (900 g) brown sugar
2 lbs. (900 g) rhubarb, chopped into 1/2-inch (1-cm) pieces
1 large fresh gingerroot, peeled and grated
1 lb. (450 g) sultana raisins
3 cloves garlic, peeled and chopped
3 lemons, thinly sliced
1/2 tsp. (2 mL) cayenne

Place the vinegar and sugar in a heavy-bottomed saucepan and bring to a boil. Add all the other ingredients and lower the heat to simmer. Cook without a lid for 2-3 hours. The chutney should be thick and dark. Put in small sterilized jars and seal. Makes 4 cups (1 L).

Carrot Marmalade

Thinly chopped rind of 1 lemon
Thinly chopped rind of 1 orange
2 1/2 cups (625 mL) cooked, finely chopped carrots
Juice of 1 lemon
Juice of 1 orange
4 cups (1 L) sugar

Boil the chopped rind in a little water until tender. Add the carrots, orange and lemon juices, and the sugar. Cook until mixture thickens, stirring frequently. Pour into sterilized jars and seal. Makes about 3 cups (750 mL).

Noël's Onion Jam

Onion jam has a rich, intense taste that goes very well with roasted meats, quiche, chicken, and cold cuts. Make it with red or yellow onions. It keeps well in the refrigerator, but it's so good that it won't last.

2 lbs. (900 g) chopped red or yellow onions
4 Tbsp. (60 mL) butter or margarine
Dash of salt
2/3 cup (150 mL) sugar
1/2 cup (125 mL) dry sherry
4 Tbsp. (60 mL) herb vinegar
1/4 cup (60 mL) honey
Freshly ground pepper
Dash of cayenne pepper

Put onions and butter or margarine in a saucepan and sauté for a few minutes. Add remaining ingredients, lower heat and simmer until the mixture has thickened, about 45 minutes. Taste for seasoning. Add more cayenne pepper if you like it hotter. Store in the refrigerator in a sterilized jar. Warm to room temperature before serving. Makes 3-4 cups (750 mL-1 L).

A Dish on the Side

ne Christmas several years ago I made a difficult decision: I decided to vary the Christmas menu. The conservative, traditional part of my soul initially screamed—no!no!—the menu must stay the same! But my low boredom threshold and lust for variety called out for new and unusual flavors, and perhaps even new traditions.

If I've learned one thing after thirty years of cooking Christmas dinners, it's the value of new traditions. And one of the most important starts with giving up the role of the martyr/victim/ super-host. This only leads to an exhausted, embittered cook who, at six o'clock, is wretched and near hysteria, clanging pots and emitting feeble cries of distress that go unheard in the living room where, in the case of my family, the assembled are quaffing champagne and scoffing my fisherman brother's divine smoked salmon.

Cooks of the world—learn to delegate and loosen your chains! Now my brother and husband prepare the smoked salmon on black bread while cousins and daughters set the table. Friends peel all the vegetables, the chef daughter makes the gravy with some of her treasured, rich brown demi-glace. The Christmas pudding, made long before, is ready and the cranberry sauce made earlier and frozen is thawed. Another guest is plunked by the fire to make the hard sauce for the pudding, dribbling in the brandy and slowly

beating the butter and icing sugar to creamy peaks. The fire burns
cheerfully, extra logs are lugged upstairs, and many candles are lit.
All afternoon there is a hustle and bustle, and I suddenly realize
that apart from the responsibility for big bird and being the bossy
administrator, all the tasks are being done by others and I am
having a good time and enjoying my Christmas afternoon.

We all take a walk down the road before dark and visit the old
1865 clapboard church nestled in the valley among the moss-hung
oaks. Big bird is almost done upon return. I cook my turkey the
old-fashioned way, rubbing it with butter and wrapping it in a piece
of clean sheet or a tea towel. I baste it through the cloth and a half-
hour before it is done I remove the sheet and finish the browning.
Hide the fat-soaked piece of sheet well in the garbage. Once my
sheepdog found it and ate half of it and, well, you can guess the
outcome for yourself. Not a very nice touch to the Christmas
celebrations.

Twice in the past twenty years we have packed up and gone to
a ski hill. On Christmas Day, everyone skied except me, for I feel it
is a rather perverse form of suicide. I stayed in bed and read my
Christmas books and got up occasionally to baste the turkey. A
pleasurable afternoon but somehow un-Christmaslike, and we had
to leave the dogs behind.

Once I had made the momentous decision to change the
Christmas menu, I spent many pleasant hours browsing through
my cookbooks. This produced some interesting new side dishes for
my family to try. I chose the usual traditional vegetables, but they
have new twists and combinations: brussels sprouts with poppy
seeds and sherry, plus a baked julienne of potatoes and celeriac, to
name just two. *The Nantucket Open House Cookbook,* by Sarah Leah

Chase, and *The Homemaker's Magazine Cookbook*, edited by Thelma
Dickman, were wonderful sources of inspiration for new takes on
the conservative Christmas vegetable.

As a veteran of many Christmas dinners, I will repeat my sage
advice: democratize and delegate dinner preparations. Allocate jobs
in a clear, commanding way. (Sometimes my family have been
heard to mutter: "She who must be obeyed.") Just before dinner,
fling off your apron, smooth your hair, and quaff some champagne.

Baked Julienne of Potatoes and Celeriac

4 large boiling potatoes, peeled and cut into thin julienne strips
3 1/2 cups (875 mL) julienned celeriac, canned or fresh
1 medium onion, chopped
3 large eggs
1 cup (250 mL) heavy cream or whipping cream
1 cup (250 mL) milk
5 oz. (150 g) St. André cheese
1 tsp. (5 mL) celery seeds
Salt and freshly ground pepper to taste
4 Tbsp. (60 mL) (1/2 stick) unsalted butter, melted

Preheat oven to 375°F (190°C). Place the julienned potatoes and celeriac in
a clean kitchen towel and squeeze out as much moisture as possible. Toss
the potatoes, celeriac, and onion together in a mixing bowl.

Beat the eggs, cream, milk, and cheese in a smaller bowl until
smooth. Season with the celery seeds, salt, and pepper.

Coat the bottom of a large gratin dish with the melted butter. Spread
the potatoes, celeriac, and onion mixture evenly in the dish, and pour the
egg mixture evenly over all.

Bake the gratin until the vegetables are tender and the top is crusty
and brown, 55-60 minutes. Let cool several minutes, then serve. Makes
10-12 servings.

Brussels Sprouts with Poppy and Sherry

1 1/2 lbs. (675 g) brussels sprouts, trimmed and cut with an X on bottom
3 Tbsp. (45 mL) unsalted butter
2 Tbsp. (30 mL) sherry
1 1/2 Tbsp. (22 mL) poppy seeds
Pinch of grated nutmeg
Salt and freshly ground pepper to taste

Steam the brussels sprouts in a vegetable steamer over boiling water just until crisp-tender. Drain.

Meanwhile, melt the butter in a small saucepan. Stir in the sherry and the poppy seeds and simmer for 3 minutes. Stir in the nutmeg, salt, and pepper to taste. Pour in the butter over the hot brussels sprouts in a serving bowl; toss to coat well. Serve at once. Makes 6 servings.

The Waiting Game

I f December is a time for wishing in the garden, January is a time for waiting. Should your character contain the virtue of patience, January will pass much more quickly. If you do not have a patient character, January can be a very difficult month, and trips to Hawaii or Mexico are in order to restore irascible temperaments to their usual mellowness.

My first urge in January is to eliminate all signs of Christmas. Out goes the tree and the dried-up boughs. Decorations are packed away. I put the poinsettias in the glass-enclosed porch, tired of their red cheerfulness. I want austerity, plainness, and bare tables and floors with pale wintry light shining on the clean surfaces. My food has to be plain also. A friend once cooked the perfect, unadorned, after-Christmas dinner, such a relief after the holiday surfeit: a New England boiled dinner with rosy pink corned beef, small perfectly boiled potatoes, boiled carrots, and crunchy-crisp boiled green cabbage. It was served on large white plates with bowls of horseradish sauce. This dinner appealed to my January sensibility. The clean taste, the unadorned vegetables, and the white plates satisfied my puritan feelings.

Walks are in order in January. We often walk on the beach after a stormy night and tuck some large garbage bags under our arms to fill up with fresh storm-tossed seaweed. We truck it home and put it on the barren-looking asparagus bed, which lies there in a January funk—dark and dormant. It is hard to believe that in four months I will be snapping off sprigs of the divine stuff. The dogs get very excited about the new smells in the garden and have green bits of seaweed sticking to their muzzles. I tuck some around the artichoke plants and feel good and nurturing like a mother feeding her child.

January brings few flowers but the ones it does bring are showboats. Our old white garage will be covered with yellow winter jasmine, the sunny blossoms a brave and valiant flag of color waving defiantly in the face of cold somber January. I pick budded branches and put them in the house where they soon bloom in the warmth, adding a touch of spring to the wintry scene. The snow-drops are all budded up and I can see them from the kitchen window. It is pleasant to be able to observe them as I wash the dishes. I gather some green moss from the woods behind the sheep pasture and make little moss gardens in low pottery dishes. Forcing some spring bulbs is quite cheering and counteracts the January blahs.

The ewes are very fat and woolly now. Lambing time is nearing—just a few more weeks. The ewes huff and puff more, and on chilly days there are little clouds of sheep breath circling their heads. There are a few Granny Smith trees in the bottom meadow, and if the winter has been mild I can pick some for the sheep (they get the scabby ones) and the kitchen gets the choice pick. If I get inspired, I make a tarte Tatin with an apricot glaze. I drive to the neighboring farm and buy a large sack of broken carrots (under five dollars) to feed to the sheep, the goat, and the donkey to give them some extra vitamins. The ewes are very spoiled with grain, green alfalfa, carrots, and apples. They hopefully will produce healthy bouncing lambs in mid-February.

The donkey has grown a wild and wiry gray winter coat. His ancestors came from Sicily and were not used to this damp wet cold. The owner of the donkey farm where Joker was born makes smart little navy raincoats with tartan linings for her precious beasts. Joker has to make do with an old shed when it rains or the comfort of some ancient, low hanging Douglas firs.

In the garden we can still dig carrots and beets for dinner. There are stored potatoes, garlic, and shallots left. This year we put rosemary, sage, and thyme leaves in the bags—supposedly to stop them from sprouting early. We shall see.

Every few years it snows and freezes up and we drag our cross-country skis out and tramp and slide across the fields making a small circuit. The sheep stare at us in wonderment. What are they doing now? The goose pond often freezes over and I take an ax to it so that the fierce ones may drink. They stand at a good distance while I wield the ax on the ice. I think they have ancestral, atavistic memories of axes and bloody finales or they have read the opening line to *Charlotte's Web*—"Where's Papa going with that ax?"

A lot of self-pruning takes place in the winter storms, and we drag the big evergreen branches to the burning pile where they will be torched later in the spring. Bays, myrtles, and rosemary are tucked away in the small unheated greenhouse. I check them to see how they are surviving the winter—monitoring their watering needs with my finger in the soil.

Another January occupation is feeding birds outside the kitchen window. The birds have long ago stripped the sunflower seeds from the garden, which were grown for them last summer. Now they consume vast amounts of store-bought sunflower seeds. The feeder is right next to the window, which is good for my nearsighted eyes. I hang the bare oak tree with seed bells and its gaunt branches are alive with flutters and twitters. When the sunflower container is empty, the birds hang onto the window demanding dinner and refills. Have patience, I call to them. January is a waiting game.

Tea time is one of the regular pleasures that get me through this long and somber month. After a brisk walk we light the fire with old apple wood, which burns like large lumps of coal. I take the best teacups out and put them on the wicker tea trolley (the silent maid). We have collected old toasting forks and ignoring my hi-tech Cuisinart programmed toaster (no romance there) we toast slices of thick whole wheat bread over the fire—now turned to hot coals. Andrew reverts back to being an English schoolboy with memories of toast and jam—the culinary high point of most boarding schools. I select a jar of last summer's best raspberry jam and we happily sit with cups of Earl Grey and toast and jam. As Laurie Colwin, the food writer and novelist, writes, tea is one of the most satisfying meals in the world (why did she die so young?). Colwin liked tea because you can ask adults and children, and the preparation can be simple: toast and jam and they're gone by six. No one needs a large dinner after that and you can go to bed early with a good book.

So there are things to do on the farm while we play the waiting game for spring. We go on walks, have tea, feed the birds regularly, read our Christmas books, and in several weeks the lambs will be born, and new chives will begin to stick their heads up. Happy New Year from Ravenhill Farm.

Here are a few recipes to make for a cozy afternoon tea on a rainy January day.

Winter Savory Stilton Biscuits

Robust Stilton cheese pairs well with the peppery, piny flavor of winter savory. You can also use rosemary. This recipe comes from my book *Winter Pleasures: Preserving and Cooking Herbs*.

3 Tbsp. (45 mL) finely chopped winter savory or rosemary
2 cups (500 mL) all-purpose flour
2 tsp. (10 mL) baking powder
1/2 tsp. (2 ml.) baking soda
1 cup (250 mL) grated Stilton cheese, or substitute sharp cheddar or blue cheese
1/2 cup (125 mL) butter or margarine
1 tsp. (5 mL) sugar
1 large egg
2/3 cup (150 mL) buttermilk

Preheat the oven to 400°F (200°C). Mix savory and dry ingredients in a bowl with the cheese. Mix in butter or margarine with your fingers until it looks like fine cornmeal. Mix sugar, egg, and buttermilk together and stir into the dry ingredients until it forms a ball.

Place the dough on a floured surface. Knead lightly a few times and roll out until it's about 1/2 an inch (1 cm) thick. Cut into rounds with a floured cutter. Place on a greased cookie sheet and bake about 18-20 minutes until the tops are lightly browned. Makes 15-18 biscuits.

Lemon Thyme Cake

This loaf cake keeps well and also freezes well. The lemon glaze adds extra lemon punch. This recipe, as well as the one that follows, comes from *Summer Delights: Growing and Cooking Fresh Herbs.*

2 cups (500 mL) unbleached flour
2 tsp. (10 mL) baking powder
Sprinkle of salt
6 Tbsp. (90 mL) softened butter
1 cup (250 mL) sugar
2 eggs
1 Tbsp. (15 mL) grated lemon zest
2 Tbsp. (30 mL) fresh lemon juice
2 Tbsp. (30 mL) chopped lemon thyme
2/3 cup (150 mL) milk
2 Tbsp. (30 mL) fresh lemon juice
1/2 cup (125 mL) icing sugar

Preheat oven to 325°F (160°C). Grease and flour a loaf pan.

Sift together flour, baking powder, and salt. In another bowl, cream the butter and beat in the sugar until fluffy. Add eggs and beat well. Stir in lemon zest, 2 Tbsp. (30 mL) lemon juice, lemon thyme, and milk. Slowly whisk in the flour mixture and mix well.

Pour into the loaf pan. Bake for 1 hour, or until a knife inserted comes out clean. Cool on a rack.

To make the lemon glaze, mix 2 Tbsp. (30 mL) lemon juice with the icing sugar so it is of a thin, pourable consistency. Pour over the cooked cake, spread with a brush, and serve. Makes 12 slices.

Rosemary-Thyme Shortbread

I found the source of this recipe in a Brooklyn Botanical Garden herb book. Serve the cookies on a plate decorated with sprigs of rosemary and lemon thyme.

1/4 cup (60 mL) icing sugar
9 Tbsp. (135 mL) soft butter
1 1/2 cups (375 mL) all-purpose flour
1 Tbsp. (15 mL) chopped fresh rosemary
1 Tbsp. (15 mL) finely chopped lemon thyme
1 Tbsp. (15 mL) granulated sugar

Preheat oven to 350°F (180°C). Combine the icing sugar and butter and mix well. Stir in the flour, rosemary, and thyme. Knead the dough a few times on a lightly floured surface. Roll out the dough to about a 1/4-inch (6-mm) thickness and cut into shapes. Bake on a greased cookie sheet until cookies are a pale gold color. Sprinkle granulated sugar on the cookies and cool on racks. Store in an airtight tin. Makes about 30 cookies.

Seedy Reading

very obsessive group in society, it seems, has a fantasy magazine or fetish catalog—cooks and gardeners included. You've seen the gastro-porn food magazines with color photographs of food oozing juices. Well, seed catalogs are gardeners' "dream" literature. The names and descriptions of the plants alone can provide a lot of entertaining reading. I once ordered a mysterious salad green from a French catalog because I was intrigued by its name—*pis en lit,* or wet your bed. Once it had grown I realized it was the dandelion and the French call it that because the leaves have diuretic properties. Most of the catalogs we use, however, come from North America and I have picked our top five.

My husband Andrew's favorite is the Territorial Seeds catalog. I think of it as very male and pragmatic. Printed on newsprint, it is straightforward, specific, and full of advice. The seeds, which will germinate vigorously and mature in a cool climate, are selected for growing in coastal B.C. They are tested in Oregon without pesticides, in ordinary soil, using only organic fertilizer. Yes, you can grow veggies year round in a B.C. garden.

The catalog contains extensive tips on growing and advice on organic fertilizers, composting, and season extenders. In fact, the seed quality and free advice alone are sufficient to build a successful garden. Each vegetable's advantages, disadvantages, and idio-syncrasies are clearly described.

Plants that look beautiful and provide you with edible delicacies are double winners for me. That is why I always order the seeds for globe artichokes, wonderful silver-green architectural plants that look good in the vegetable or flower garden. I also love Territorial's 'Royal Burgundy' beans, which produce purple pods that turn magically green when cooked—a built-in blanching signal. Purple sprouting broccoli is another favorite. Planted in late summer, it winters over and in March and April blossoms forth with beautiful purple florets that are sweet and crunchy.

Another Territorial favorite is 'Lollo Rossa', a pretty, frilly red lettuce that makes a charming border in the garden as well as a sprightly salad or garnish. A silver salmon laid on a bed of 'Lollo Rossa' is a cook's delight. 'Little Gem', a mini-romaine, is another small treasure for your salad garden.

We have also found melons that will grow on the coast in the Territorial catalog. Andrew helps out melons by putting them in plastic cold frames, which ups the heat quotient. Eggplants and peppers also grow happily in these boxes.

There is a good selection of herb seeds, such as dill and cilantro varieties that are slow to bolt, and seven kinds of basil.

Territorial's seeds and catalog are available by writing 206-8475 Ontario Street, Vancouver, B.C. V5X 3E8.

 Shepherds Garden Seeds is the creation of Renee Shepherd from Felton, California, and, in sharp contrast to Territorial, is a feminine seed catalog, illustrated with charming line drawings and soft-focus watercolors. Shepherd visits seed growers all over Europe and procures seeds that produce vegetables bred for flavor and not size. Here you will find tiny French haricot beans, baby beets from Holland, French flageolets, Italian broccoli, specialty corn (even popcorn), cornichons for your pâté, watercress, and a brilliant and varied lettuce collection.

I enjoy summer salads made of butterhead lettuces and the names are irresistible: 'Capitaine', 'Juliet', 'Mantilla'. Their smooth, buttery flavors need just a touch of good olive oil and a splash of herb vinegar. The pale tender hearts of these lettuces are perfect and are rarely available at the grocers. 'Tom Thumb' is a charming little English heirloom lettuce that makes your garden look like a Peter Rabbit patch. Each head is the perfect size for an individual salad. There is also arugula, also called rocket or roquette, that peppery, spicy green to which one can become addicted. Easy to grow and a self-seeder, it can become a permanent fixture in your garden and your salad bowl.

Corn salad or mâche, available in the catalog, winters over in a coastal garden. We eat it in February every year. It is a sweet green mild leaf that is planted in late summer and grows through the fall and winter.

If you have ever eaten mesclun salad in the south of France and yearn to repeat the experience, here is your chance. Shepherds has unique mesclun salad mixes that are cut-and-come-again greens. They are a mix of young salad greens, many with a sharp piquant taste.

There is also a selection of Asian greens. Last year we planted the red mustard that gives a Dijon-like lift to salads or ham sandwiches. It seeded itself and grew all winter and spring. Not only was it an asset to my kitchen, it made a cheerful splash of red in the garden.

Shepherds also specializes in culinary herbs and does a wonderful job with unique seeds, advice, and recipes. Besides the usual culinary herbs, there is a herbal tea collection, a new creeping edible thyme, and a page of Italian basils whose names will roll off your tongue: 'Basil Genova Profumatissima', 'Basil Napoletano', 'Basil Fino Verde Compatto'. Saying their names out loud is almost as much fun as growing and eating them. There is also lettuce-leaf basil with large leaves you can wrap food in, purple-opal basil, anise basil, Greek mini window box and lemon basil.

The edible flower section lists anise hyssop, borage, Johnny-jump-ups, calendulas, chive blossoms, lemon gem marigolds, and four types of nasturtiums. All these flowers are easy and satisfying to grow and will beautify your summer meals and garden.

Shepherds Seeds is illustrated with lovely line drawings of vegetables, flowers, and herbs, boxed recipes and growing advice. Renee Shepherd has written two cookbooks called *Recipes from a Kitchen Garden, Vols. 1 and 2,* which I highly recommend and use every summer. They are filled with simple recipes using fresh produce and are inspired by many ethnic cultures.

Write to Shepherds Garden Seeds, 30 Irene Street, Torrington, Connecticut 06790 for a free catalog. Once you have received your catalog, you can telephone and place credit card orders.

 Two other herb catalogs worth sending for are Richters and Nichols Garden Nursery. Richters has an extensive selection of herb seeds, both culinary and medicinal, and is full of information on the uses of herbs. They have fourteen types of basil to tantalize your taste buds, eight kinds of parsley, nine types of rosemary, and eighteen sages. Plants as well as seed are available and are shipped in May. Cooks will also like the selection of gourmet vegetables. There's a new asparagus called 'Jersey Centennial', oriental cucumbers, celeriac, daikon radish, gai lohn (Chinese broccoli), Belgian endive, orach, purslane, and shungiku (an edible chrysanthemum). Write to Richters Herb Catalogue, Goodwood, Ontario L0C 1A0.

Oregon's Nichols Garden Nursery tests its seed for a cool maritime climate and has a long list of vegetable seeds that would please an imaginative, adventurous cook: broccoli raab, oriental vegetable salsify, yardlong beans, cardoons, chicory, corn salad, and arugula. If you live in Canada, remember that seeds from U.S. catalogs are easily ordered with no customs problems, unlike plants, which cannot be shipped to Canada. Write to Nichols Garden Nursery, 1190 North Pacific Highway, Albany, Oregon 97321-4598.

 The last top-five catalog is The Cook's Garden Seeds and Supplies for the New American Kitchen Garden published by Ellen and Shepherd Ogden, who began as market gardeners. This is where I got my first French lettuce and arugula seeds. The Ogdens travel to Europe looking for delicious herbs and vegetables. Recent discoveries have included a red-leafed smoky fennel, Dutch krausa parsley, and an Italian chard called 'Monstruoso' with a thick white rib for stir-fries or crudités. There is a cauliflower called 'Violet Queen' with a deep purple central head, golden beets, plus seven pages of various lettuces that should be enough for any salad fanatic. There are summer lettuces, year-round collections, a spring mix, and lettuces for greenhouse forcing. I am again seduced by the names as well as the tastes: 'Lollo Biondo', pale green cousin of 'Lollo Rossa'; 'Brunia', a red oak leaf; 'Esmerelda', a green butterhead, and 'North Pole', a pale green butterhead for winter growing. Cook's calls itself the salad lover's catalog and earns its boast.

The Ogdens have also compiled an excellent list of exotic salad greens and mesclun mixes accompanied by tips on growing orach, plantain, purslane, dandelion, miner's lettuce, mustard, and corn salad—all greens our pioneer ancestors used to gather in the wild and which we can now cultivate to add tang to our lettuce salads.

The catalog is beautifully illustrated with woodcuts by Mary Azarian of Vermont who has done a famous alphabet book. Her style captures the essence of country life and makes the catalog nourishing aesthetically was well as nutritionally. Write Cook's Garden, P.O. Box 535, Londonderry, Vermont 05148.

Sober-up Soups

he last few weeks, while thinking about writing this article, I've had little soup songs humming through my brain, such as the one from Alice and Maurice Sendak's enchanting hymn to chicken soup:

In January it's so nice
While slipping on the sliding ice
To sip hot chicken soup with rice
Sipping once—sipping twice
Sipping chicken soup with rice.

Oliver Twist's famous plaintive request for more gruel has also flashed through my head while I've stirred soups for the evening. I have tried to imagine who made the first soup, and my scenario takes place in a neolithic cave on the edge of the Mediterranean. A large venison bone is left outside the cave in a primitive clay container. It rains, there is nothing for dinner, and the ever-frugal cave wife heats up the bone for another gnaw. She licks her fingers, likes the taste of the transformed rainwater and . . . voilà, the first stock and soup is made. The next time she throws in a sprig of wild thyme and marjoram and the rest is history.

Soup is historically a wonderful restorative. A famous soup from Provence is called *aigo bouido,* a herb and garlic broth that is called in translation, "Save your life soup." It cures exhaustion and overindulgence and the ingredients are water, garlic, bay leaves, orange rind, sage, thyme, and pepper.

Patience Gray, whose enchanting book about peasant cookery in Europe, *Honey from a Weed,* describes a shepherd's soup from Catalan. A bunch of thyme is infused in boiling water and then poured over thin slices of bread soaked in olive oil.

The old culinary cliché of a stockpot on the back of the stove was probably very practical in the days of no refrigeration. Today, you can buy ready-made beef, veal, chicken, or vegetarian stock, fresh, frozen, or canned, or you can make stock yourself and freeze it. Bouillon cubes and canned stock can be too salty, but there are promising signs that the soup companies are coming out with low-sodium stocks and soups.

So what soup can I make from my garden in January? I pull on my gumboots and slicker and walk down the path to the cold, dismal winter garden to see what is growing there that might inspire me. Squelching around the garden like a true hunter-gatherer, I see some bright green sorrel leaves in the gloom, and over in a corner is another green flag waving at me—a patch of Italian parsley.

I pick the greens and then go to the barn to check the storage larder. There are string bags of onions, there are parsnips, and of course baskets of potatoes. Here I decide on my three soup recipes—I will make French onion soup, sorrel and potato soup, parsnip and potato soup. All are nourishing, restorative, and delicious, and can be made and frozen before the ski weekend or winter hike. Then they just need heating and garnishing with homemade croutons, chopped parsley or cilantro, and grated Parmesan. Big loaves of crusty bread complete the picture. Some wide-mouth thermoses can be useful if you want to take the soup up the ski hill or on the trail, or have a big soup tureen for the ski chalet.

Julia Child has an excellent soup chapter in *The Way To Cook*. She suggests that soup is a nutritious and frugal way to take the edge off youthful, jockish appetites—especially ones just off the ski hill.

A memorable soup of my northern Vancouver Island childhood was the giant pot of turkey soup that my mother faithfully made on New Year's Eve, when the whole village came to our house for a party. After midnight, no one was allowed to leave the house without finishing a big bowl of what we kids dubbed "Mother's Sober-Up Soup."

So here are three soups to take to the mountains from the winter vegetable garden, and as Maurice Sendak sings:

> *Happy once,*
>   *happy thrice,*
> *Happy chicken soup*
>   *with rice.*

Sorrel and Potato Soup

1 1/2 lb. (675 g) peeled and chopped potatoes
1 lb. (450 g) sorrel leaves with ribs removed
1 cup (250 mL) chopped leeks or onions
2 Tbsp. (30 mL) butter or margarine
6 cups (1.5 L) chicken stock
Freshly ground pepper and salt to taste
1 cup (250 mL) cream—heavy or light

Peel and chop the potatoes in chunks. Place in water. Take ribs from the
sorrel leaves and shred. Cook leeks or onions in the butter in a frying pan
until limp. In a pot, place the potatoes, the stock, and the sorrel and leeks
and cook for 15-20 minutes until tender. Purée in a food processor. Return
to the saucepan, taste, and add salt and pepper. Whisk in cream. Freeze or
serve garnished with chopped parsley or croutons. Serves 4-6.

French Onion Soup

3 lbs. (1.5 kg) cooking onions
6 Tbsp. (90 mL) butter
2 Tbsp. (30 mL) sugar
Salt to taste
3 Tbsp. (45 mL) flour
8 cups (2 L) beef stock
1 cup (250 mL) dry white wine or vermouth
6-8 slices toasted French bread
Grated Swiss cheese for garnish

Finely slice the onions. Cook with the butter in a heavy saucepan. Stir and
mix well and cook over low heat for 15-20 minutes, covered. Stir
occasionally; add sugar and salt and cook over low heat for 30 minutes
until the onions look brown and caramelized. Add the flour and mix well.
Now stir in the beef stock and wine. Bring to a boil and simmer for 30
minutes. Taste for seasoning. Add a splash of brandy if you wish. In each
bowl, place a piece of toasted French bread and pass the bowl of grated
Swiss cheese. This soup can be easily frozen after the last cooking. Serves 4.

Parsnip and Potato Soup with Bay and Parsley

Parsnip has a sweet earthy flavor that makes it a favorite winter vegetable.
With chicken stock and cream, it makes a wonderful soup.

8 medium to large parsnips, peeled and cut in rounds
4 medium potatoes, peeled and thinly sliced
2 medium onions, peeled and finely chopped
4 cups (1 L) chicken stock
2 bay leaves
2 cups (500 mL) light cream
Freshly ground pepper
Dash of salt
1/2 cup (125 mL) chopped parsley

Put parsnips, potatoes, onions, chicken stock, and bay leaves in a large
saucepan. Bring to a boil and simmer for 30 minutes, or until all the
vegetables are tender.

Remove bay leaves and purée vegetables in a food processor. Return
to the soup pot and whisk in the cream. Add some pepper and salt, if
desired. Heat through and sprinkle with chopped parsley before serving.
Serves 4-6.

My soup making and vegetable cooking have been greatly enhanced by
Marion Morash's *The Victory Garden Cookbook*. I recommend it to anyone
who grows vegetables or wants to cook vegetables. This book is a
correspondence course supreme in the art of vegetable cooking.

That Little Island Vineyard

On a crisp cold January morning, the garden tipped with white frost, we rose early, had a quick breakfast, pushed the excited dogs into the truck, and rushed to the Brentwood Bay ferry. A rare sight was awaiting us at the dock. Instead of the usual waves and dark sea, the bay was partially frozen and the seagulls were sitting on the ice looking slightly puzzled. Two swans were pushing their way through the ice—the most elegant icebreakers I had ever seen.

The intrepid little Brentwood Bay ferry, which I have been riding since I was a child, plowed its way through the slushy ice and soon we were at Mill Bay heading up the highway to the Venturi-Schulze Vineyard. A winery? On Vancouver Island? I was born on the Island and always assumed that wine came from elsewhere—not from our cool, gray, rainy shores. The fact is there are now four licensed vineyards on Vancouver Island.

I had first met the owners of this one at a dinner organized by the Empress Hotel for Anita Stewart, a Canadian cookbook and travel writer with a passion for Canadian food and local ingredients. Here I had met Marilyn Schulze-Venturi and Giordano Venturi, who had come to present their wines to the assemblage. During the dinner the guests sampled the Venturis' Brut Naturel '91, a Madeleine Sylvaner '93, and a vertical tasting of their extraordinary balsamic vinegars: a '92, an '87 and a '70, which is the year

Giordano first began to make his balsamic vinegars, always in the traditional way.

All the vinegars had a complex rich flavor; the older they were the more the flavor deepened and resonated on the tongue. The Brut, in an elegant bottle with a black label, is 80 percent Pinot Auxerrois, 15 percent Chasselas, and 5 percent Pinot Gris and was to be the surprise treat of the evening.

Marilyn gave a charming and passionate speech about the wine, and then and there I knew I was looking forward to the time when I would meet this woman again. Vancouver Island, she told us, gives the Brut a more austere, steely character, contributing subtlety and structure to the wine. The touch of Pinot Gris added softness and fruit to the blend with its grapefruit flavors. It was paired with roast quail at the dinner, which admirably showed off its potential. The Brut is not just a dessert wine. Though it was also paired with chocolate truffles at the Empress dinner, customers have told Marilyn that they have sipped it with everything from lobster to ice cream.

The event had made me want to visit the vineyard so I was very happy to be doing so. As you pull off the highway you find yourself in a grove of old maples. The first glimpse one gets is the winery building painted gray and the hundred-year-old farmhouse, which is in the middle of renovations and transformations. A small store has been built at the base of the house and up the steps one enters an enormous room with a monolithic fireplace. French doors face the sloping vineyard, its neat bare vines of winter all espaliered on wire divided by vivid green paths of chickweed, which will later be dug under. The Venturis greet us, pour coffee and we all sit at the dining room table. And thus begins one of the most intense and interesting wine seminars I have ever attended.

The two qualities that emanate from Marilyn and Giordano are intelligence and passion. As they begin to tell their story, they pass the conversation back and forth to each other like graceful tennis players. Occasionally I ask a question and scribble notes, but nothing breaks the flow of conversation, which continues on with intensity and drama. Little Giordana colors and draws at the next table. She is already working in the vineyard along with the older children.

The vineyard is the family's whole life and certainly this is a time-honored tradition in Europe, where family-run wineries pass from generation to generation. The French concept of terroir also enters the conversation. The earth the grapes are grown in gives it the flavor and the Venturis feel their sloping clay hill, where the vines grow very deeply and are not irrigated, can produce grapes with exceptional flavor. As they talk about the work I realize how much goes into the producing of their wine. Practically everything is done by hand, but guiding the hands are two scientifically trained brains that are always observing, monitoring, testing, and changing methods to improve their vines and their wine.

Giordano was raised in Italy near Modena where he said his father made not very good wine. Marilyn is from Australia and immigrated to B.C. as a teenager. She trained as a microbiologist and is building a laboratory in the winery. Giordano was an electronics designer and technical school teacher and planted vines in his Vancouver garden for twenty years before creating the vineyard.

The Venturis discussed how labor intensive their work is; because Vancouver Island is both wet and temperate, the vines have unusual vigor and must be pruned and tied up constantly in the growing season. Their aim is to create a sustainable vineyard that is

still producing in fifty years and will perhaps find their grand-
children working it as they sit on the porch and look at the fruits of
their labors.

Both have strong environmental concerns and grow all their
grapes without pesticides or herbicides. And while they could make
twice as much wine, it would not have the same high quality.
Marilyn goes through the vines in summer meticulously thinning
the grapes to leave only those that have the most intense flavor.
Their production is small and sells out quickly and people are
willing to pay good prices for the wine, although making money is
not the driving force behind the Venturis. It is the idea of a quality
that they are always testing, judging, and changing to improve.

The couple laughingly admit they have a strong streak of
stubbornness in both of their characters and will not sacrifice
quality for quantity and financial reward. The Empress Hotel,
Sooke Harbour House, and Harvest Moon Cafe are their firm island
supporters. Now more restaurants want their wines, and Marilyn
insists that the wine buyers visit the winery and investigate their
product before she sells it to them.

We get up from the table and stretch after our wine seminar
and walk out to the vineyard. They show us where they cleared the
land and how they milled the cut wood to incorporate into the
house renovation. They sometimes think of leasing or buying more
land, but then they think about whether they could give the
expanded vineyard the same care and love and create the same
handcrafted product.

The two lead us proudly on a tour of the winery building, a
building of many different rooms, levels, and temperatures. I am
surprised how simple much of the equipment looks. Giordano,

with his engineering and adaptive skills, is able to invent and reinvent equipment from older components, an important talent when machinery can be so expensive. Lunch follows: cheese, apples, prosciutto, salami, and Italian bread rolls made by Giordano. Simple flavorful food that does not outshine the star of the meal, a white wine called Pignoletto Aromatico 1993.

The wine is the result of an experiment using two varieties— Ortega and Schönburger. Giordano said it fell apart at bottling, but four months later that flavor surpassed all expectations. He has since proclaimed it the best white they have ever made and together they named it Pignoletto Aromatico. Pignoletto means small pinecone and refers to the shape of the grape bunches. This is not an insipid wine but bold with tropical fruit flavors and a hit of spice. It should be kept at least six months and is higher in alcohol (12.7 percent) than most white wines. The next wine we taste is a white wine of intense flavor and richness. The name of the wine, La Rocca, commemorates an old castle built in 1220 in Spilamberto, Italy. The sweet wine contains grape juice concentrated over an open fire, then fermented in barrels. It is very rich and dense and a thimbleful would revive one on a low afternoon.

Sales of the '93 vintage have been so good there is little left. A devoted list of customers have their names now tucked away for winter. Another creation of the Venturi-Schulze family is the newsletter. It is vividly written and the two personalities of Marilyn and Giordano are apparent in their writings. The reader gets an insight into their lives as they discuss all aspects of the vineyard: planting, weeding, pruning, weather watching, picking, and winemaking. If readers want to be on the mailing list, write to

Venturi-Schulze Vineyards, 4235 Trans-Canada Highway, R.R. 1, Cobble Hill, B.C. V0R 1L0. Phone/fax (604) 743-5630.

Sitting on the ferry going home I saw the swans still pushing against the slushy ice but now my mind was filled with new wine terms such as riddling (coaxing the yeast sediment to the capped end of the bottle), with the smell of balsamic vinegar, with the tastes of Pignoletto Aromatico, but mostly with the vivid impression Marilyn and Giordano had left. My name will be on their customer list and I look forward with pleasure to observing the journey of these two winemakers through the years.

Growing Wine Grapes

Yes, it is possible to grow high quality wine grapes in coastal British Columbia. Possible but difficult. Here are some guidelines for home gardeners. (If you want to grow wine grapes in other regions of North America, you will need to experiment and consult with your local nursery.)

Grape varieties must be chosen carefully, but it takes experiments over time to find out which are best suited to your soil and microclimate. Venturi-Schulze grows Madeleine Sylvaner, Madeleine Angevine, Siegerrebe, Schönburger, Pinot Noir, Pinot Auxerrois, Chasselas, Pinot Gris, Müller-Thurgau, Gewürztraminer, and Ortega.

A clay soil, with good drainage on a slope, may be the best soil for your vines. Sand or gravel subsoils have poor water retention and force irrigation, which may increase your yield but frequently decreases the quality of the grapes.

The great vigor of coastal vines means that the summer pruning of branches, the tying back of branches and wide vine spacing (8 feet/2.4 m) of plants are all important for increasing air circulation and preventing fungus disease. Cutting late developing grape branches may be necessary to direct the energy of the vine to ripening the earliest forming branches.

Crown gall, a common problem, is hard to avoid but can be

controlled by growing two or more main trunks, one being cut out when a gall develops. It is possible to order cuttings that have been tested virus-free and it is also possible to heat treat the cuttings to kill the crown gall bacterium.

Mildew is controlled by the spraying of sulphur. Weeds are forked and hand-pulled, except for chickweed, which is allowed to grow between the rows of vines to prevent erosion from winter rain. The entire vineyard is enclosed with nets to prevent bird damage as the grapes ripen. Deer fencing is also a necessity in many rural areas.

—Andrew Yeoman

Index to Recipes

Index to Gardening Tips